"*The Depression Solutions Workbook* includes tested me............................... ..s
a tremendous resource for clinicians and clients alike."

—Thorana S. Nelson, Ph.D., professor of family therapy at Utah State University

The Depression Solutions Workbook

A STRENGTHS & SKILLS-BASED APPROACH

JACQUELINE CORCORAN, PH.D.

New Harbinger Publications, Inc.

Publisher's Note

This publication is designed to provide accurate and authoritative information in regard to the subject matter covered. It is sold with the understanding that the publisher is not engaged in rendering psychological, financial, legal, or other professional services. If expert assistance or counseling is needed, the services of a competent professional should be sought.

Corcoran, *Mental Health in Social Work: Casebook on Diagnosis & Strengths*, p. 189, © 2009. Reproduced by permission of Pearson Education, Inc.

Bertolino, COLLABORATIVE COMPETENCY BASED COUNSELING & THERAPY, *pp. 76 and 77, © 2002. Reproduced by permission of Pearson Education, Inc.*

Acquired by Melissa Kirk; Cover design by Amy Shoup;
Edited by Nelda Street; Text design by Tracy Carlson

Library of Congress Cataloging-in-Publication Data on file with the publisher

11 10 09

10 9 8 7 6 5 4 3 2 1   First printing

To Mark

Contents

• A Strengths and Skills Based Approach • About the Author • How This Book
Is Organized

PART I
Building Strengths

CHAPTER 1

• Symptoms of Depression • Dealing with Your Depression • Putting It
All Together: A Plan for Coping • Conclusion

CHAPTER 2

• Risk and Protective Factors for Depression • Finding Resilience in Other Areas
of Your Life • Putting It All Together • Conclusion

PART II
Building Motivation

PART III
Building Skills

Acknowledgments

To the staff at New Harbinger, especially Melissa Kirk, Jess Beebe, and Nelda Street, for their support and professionalism as I developed this workbook. I also wanted to thank the following former students for their contributions to case material: Angela Corriveau, Rosalind Frazer, Rosita Kline, Amantha Peterson, Janice Reeves, Sarah Roenfeldt, and Mary VanWyngarden.

Introduction

Depression is the most common mental illness, afflicting 17 percent of the U.S. population at some point in their lifetimes (Kessler et al. 2003). This figure represents tens of millions of people, so you're not alone. If you've picked up this book, you probably suspect that you're depressed. What are the symptoms?

According to the *Diagnostic and Statistical Manual of Mental Disorders* (*DSM*) of the American Psychiatric Association (2000), which is the standard resource for mental health diagnosis in the United States, three different disorders represent depressive symptoms: major depressive disorder, dysthymic disorder, and adjustment disorder with depressed mood. *Major depressive disorder* is a period of two weeks or longer during which a person experiences a depressed mood or loss of interest in nearly all life activities. *Dysthymic disorder* represents a general personality style featuring symptoms that are similar to, but less intense than, those of major depression. In a given year, 1.5 percent of the adult population will suffer from dysthymic disorder (Kessler et al. 2003). *Adjustment disorder with depressed mood* represents depressive symptoms that develop from a person's response to an identifiable stressor, such as a divorce, a job loss, or a move. To qualify for this diagnosis, the symptoms must begin within three months of the stressor; they usually don't persist any longer than six months; and the person's job, academic, or social functioning must be temporarily impaired in significant ways. You'll find checklists for symptoms of depression in chapter 1.

What are the consequences of being depressed? You may already experience some of them, and they include:

- Isolation

- Employment problems

- Marital problems

- Parenting problems

- Suicidal thoughts or acts

- Health problems

More specifically, depression can be detrimental to physical health, contributing to lack of movement, more illnesses and doctor visits, and even early death. If you already have a medical illness (and people with illnesses and disability are at increased risk for depression), untreated depression can block recovery as well as your motivation and ability to follow through with prescribed treatment.

Finally, although depression often gets better after one episode, it's also common for it to follow a chronic, relapsing, or recurrent course. **That is, after one episode of depression, many people go on to have more episodes, even though they may recover in between.**

As you can see, depression is a serious problem, and it's important to tackle it, rather than wait to see if it will fade on its own. *The Depression Solutions Workbook: A Strengths and Skills-Based Approach* will help you do just that.

A STRENGTHS AND SKILLS BASED APPROACH

Following is a very brief description of each of the three theoretical approaches underlying *The Depression Solutions Workbook*: solution-focused therapy, motivational interviewing, and cognitive behavioral therapy. Then I'll show how the workbook is organized.

Solution-Focused Therapy

Solution-focused therapy, developed by Steve de Shazer, Insoo Kim Berg, Michelle Weiner-Davis, and colleagues (1986), focuses on a person's strengths, abilities, and other resources, helping the person discover and build upon these resources.

Twenty years ago, when solution-focused therapy was first developed, this was a revolutionary concept: to work on what the person was doing well, not what was wrong with him. Solution-focused therapy is based on the idea that change can occur rapidly, and that even a small change can lead to a "spiral effect." The person takes a step in the right direction, prompting others around him to respond differently, which in turn makes him feel more empowered, encouraging further steps toward change. For example, suppose an older woman with depression motivates herself to get dressed and go for a walk so that the fresh air and exercise might give her more energy. Because she's up and around, she might run into a neighbor who responds in a friendly fashion. Then, feeling slightly better from the walk and social interaction, the woman may feel motivated to make a phone call to a recreation center to find out about local senior activities.

Both behaving differently and thinking differently are part of the processes of change (de Shazer 1994). In solution-focused therapy, people are considered the experts on themselves and are encouraged to find the solutions that are right for them. Discovering their own strengths mobilizes them to apply these strengths to problem situations.

The solution-focused techniques presented in this workbook will help you identify:

- What *is* working well in your life

- What you do differently during depression-free times

- The strengths you've developed as a result of your mood problems

- How you've managed to cope with hardships

Although you may currently feel hopeless about the future, solution-focused techniques will help you visualize a nondepressed future, which you can then start working toward.

Motivational Interviewing

Motivational interviewing, created by William R. Miller and Stephen Rollnick (2002), is a short-term approach that focuses on building motivation for change. It's rooted in the idea that ambivalence toward change—wanting to change but also being stuck in the problem—is a natural process. Like solution-focused therapy, motivational interviewing helps you develop hope and vision about the possibility of change. Techniques will focus on helping you see why it might be a good idea to go ahead and make changes, even while still working on identifying some of the reasons why depression might actually be meeting some of your needs. Motivational interviewing techniques in this workbook will help you:

- Bolster your motivation to overcome your depression.

- Examine any unhealthy coping methods, such as substance use, or excessive eating or television watching, that you've adopted to manage your depression.

Cognitive Behavioral Therapy

In *cognitive behavioral therapy*, the nature of change is apparent in its name. That is, you can change in the following ways (Young et al. 2007):

- Cognitively, by identifying and changing distorted thinking

- Behaviorally, by learning skills to improve your coping capacities

The cognitive behavioral techniques presented in this book include problem solving, daily scheduling of pleasant activities, and communication skills training. Chapter 8 attacks belief systems that create and sustain depression.

However, cognitive behavioral therapy is an approach that's best implemented when people are in the "action" stage of change, according to the Transtheoretical Stages of Change Model (Prochaska, Norcross, and DiClemente 1994). Before people can take action, they first need to feel motivated to change. This book will help you build your motivation as well as your appreciation and knowledge of your own strengths, so you can then start to use cognitive behavioral techniques to take constructive actions that will help you recover from depression.

ABOUT THE AUTHOR

I've been a practicing psychotherapist since 1994, and I earned my master's degree in social work in 1989. I received a Ph.D. in 1996 from the University of Texas and, since then, have served as a faculty member in two different universities, the University of Texas at Arlington and Virginia Commonwealth University, where I currently work.

As a result of my work, I wrote *Building Strengths and Skills: A Collaborative Approach to Working with Clients* (Oxford University Press, 2004), a book on how to integrate with cognitive behavioral therapy the strengths-based approaches I discuss in this workbook. I've had a lot of success with this integration in my practice, especially when seeing clients who have depression. That's why I decided to write this workbook, to offer ways for people suffering from depression to help themselves using the techniques and exercises I developed.

HOW THIS BOOK IS ORGANIZED

The main focus of *The Depression Solutions Workbook* is on brief explanations of techniques, along with case examples. I invite you to write in your own responses to the exercises that follow each technique. I also provide abundant case examples so that you can see how other people have used the techniques. These examples will illustrate some common types of life situations that contribute to depression, such as childhood abuse, domestic violence, and loss of relationships.

This book will help you identify, reinforce, and strengthen your own personal strengths, resources, and motivations. You'll use cognitive behavioral skill-building to bolster areas where you have knowledge, or improve skill gaps that seem to interfere with your functioning. *The Depression Solutions Workbook* provides exercises that will help you become attuned to your unique strengths and resources, which will cause you to start feeling better about yourself, adopting a more positive worldview, and feeling more empowered to make use of cognitive behavioral strategies to "beat your depression."

PART I

Building Strengths

CHAPTER 1

Finding Your Strengths: Coping

If you're depressed, you may have lost sight of your personal resources in terms of attitudes, beliefs, abilities, qualities, behaviors, and supports. This chapter will begin the process of helping you explore your strengths, starting with how you use them to cope with your depression. In this process, you'll discover that you're more actively engaged in solving your problems and managing your depression than you believed. Research has identified an active problem-solving style as a positive coping mechanism to prevent depression (Holahan et al. 2005).

SYMPTOMS OF DEPRESSION

When depression hits, most people have difficulty thinking about anything except how bad they feel. Because of this tendency, let's start by looking at the symptoms themselves. Although completing the following checklists doesn't lead to a formal diagnosis of depression (only a mental health professional can make a diagnosis), doing so will give you a general sense of what your depressive symptoms are and their level of intensity. As mentioned in the introduction, there are three types of depression that can be diagnosed, as categorized by the *Diagnostic and Statistical Manual of Mental Disorders* (*DSM*) of the American Psychiatric Association (the official manual for diagnosis in the United States): major depressive disorder, adjustment disorder with depressed mood, and dysthymic disorder.

Major Depressive Disorder

Put a check mark next to any of these symptoms you've had every day or almost every day for at least two weeks:

CHECKLIST

Symptoms of Major Depressive Disorder	√
Do you experience a depressed mood most of the day?	
Do you have less interest or pleasure lately in the types of activities you used to enjoy?	
Without trying, have you suffered significant weight loss, or put on weight? Have you had an increase or a decrease in appetite?	
Do you have difficulty falling asleep, or do you wake up in the middle of the night unable to get back to sleep? Do you sleep much more than you used to?	
Do you feel tired or "slowed down"?	
Do you feel worthless or guilt ridden?	
Do you have problems thinking or concentrating?	
Do you think about death or suicide, or have you actually made an attempt?	

If you answered yes to at least five of these questions, you may have major depressive disorder.

Adjustment Disorder with Depressed Mood

Adjustment disorders are diagnosed when people become depressed in response to some identifiable, recent life stressor, such as a romantic breakup, a move, or a change in jobs. As previously mentioned, to qualify for this diagnosis the symptoms must begin within three months of the stressor, and they usually don't persist longer than six months. If you've suffered from a recent stressful life event and have less than five of the symptoms presented for major depressive disorder, then you may have an adjustment disorder with depressed mood.

Dysthymic Disorder

Dysthymic disorder is a chronic (lasting at least two years) low-level depression that's experienced more days than not. Put a check mark next to any of the following symptoms you've experienced over the last two-year period.

CHECKLIST

Symptoms of Dysthymic Disorder	√
Do you have a poor appetite, or do you overeat?	
Do you have trouble sleeping, or do you sleep too much?	
Do you have low energy or tiredness?	
Do you suffer from low self-esteem?	
Do you have poor concentration or difficulty making decisions?	
Do you feel hopeless?	

If you checked more than two of these symptoms for a two-year period, you may be suffering from dysthymic disorder.

Although you can't diagnose yourself with a clinical disorder, using the checklists may give you some idea of the symptoms that encompass depression and your experience of them. As a result of completing the checklists, you may choose to visit a mental health professional, either a psychiatrist or a psychotherapist. If you have the majority of the symptoms listed for major depressive disorder and symptoms have been present for a significant period of time (such as three months), you're probably in a lot of psychological pain and could benefit from some immediate relief. Additionally, I would be concerned if you're contemplating suicide, particularly if the symptoms have gone on for some time. In this case, you might also benefit from some face-to-face professional guidance in managing your pain. However, no matter what kind of depressive disorder you may have, you can benefit from this book and use it whether or not you decide to work with a professional.

■ *Case Example: Tammy*

Tammy is a forty-four-year-old African American female who was diagnosed with multiple sclerosis (MS), a degenerative autoimmune disease, nearly fifteen years ago. The disease has progressed to the point where she walks with two canes, one in each hand. Tammy can't hold a job because of her disability, and receives about five hundred dollars from Supplemental Security Income (SSI) each month. She also receives food stamps and Medicaid.

Tammy has shared a basement bedroom with a friend for the past eighteen months. The friend's grown son, who doesn't live with them, owns the house. The friend also has two other sons who live in the house. Tammy pays them a rent of two hundred dollars each month, and uses her food stamps to buy food for the entire household. The situation stresses her significantly, because the two young men make her feel unwanted. They're loud, and they harass her, making it difficult for her to sleep. She can't use the shower, because it's not big enough for her safety seat and she's fallen a few times while showering, so she takes sponge baths in her room instead.

The stress of the situation worries her, increasing her fear that she'll have another attack of MS and require hospitalization. She's been hospitalized once since moving in with this friend. Now, for the past several weeks, she's found herself crying every day, feeling hopeless, and wanting to hurt herself. She's never actually attempted self-harm, however. She stays in her bed, either sleeping or watching television most days, except for when she has her physical therapy appointments. She describes feeling "incredibly tired" and also says that she wants to stay out of the way of her roommates so they won't bother her.

When she uses the symptom checklists, Tammy finds that she seems to meet the criteria for major depressive disorder. For the last several weeks, nearly every day she has had a depressed mood, diminished interest or pleasure in activities, increased sleep, fatigue and energy loss, and thoughts of self-harm.

DEALING WITH YOUR DEPRESSION

Now that you've considered your symptoms of depression, you'll be asked about the ways you've dealt with them. What do you do when you feel really bad? In psychological terms, the way people deal with their problems is referred to as *coping*. Some people stay in bed all day; others prefer to be alone. Still others spend their time watching television. Some people overeat, or use drugs or alcohol to seek relief. These types of methods involve *negative*, or *unhealthy*, *coping mechanisms*.

Other people exercise, call people they're close to, write in a journal, or distract themselves with hobbies. These are considered *positive*, or *healthy*, *ways of coping*. Typically, people do more than one thing when they feel depressed, using both positive and negative ways to deal with depression. For example, Peter plays video games for hours at a time when he feels depressed. Although distraction can be a helpful way to cope, doing something to the exclusion of other important activities can be unhelpful. Peter also spends time with his wife, who helps him remember that he's loved, and he keeps up in communicating with his daughter, who lives in another state. The relationship with his daughter keeps him from only thinking about his emotional pain.

Doing the Exercises

Before getting started with the first exercise, let's cover some typical reactions people with depression have to doing exercises. Some people don't have the energy or don't want to make the effort. If this is your tendency, only take on one exercise at a time to avoid becoming overwhelmed. Some exercises have more than one question, so if you even manage to answer one part, validate yourself for making progress. Just working on the exercises a little each day and assessing the impact of that work on your mood will mean that you're taking action to beat your depression.

Another useful technique for people who have a hard time starting a task is to only commit five minutes to a task. After five minutes, give yourself permission to stop. You'll be surprised at how much you can do in five minutes, and you may even want to continue after that point.

Other people, when faced with an exercise, may draw a blank. Part of this tendency may be from the fear of failure that depressed people often feel; unless you have the "right" answer, you may feel that you're a terrible and unworthy person. But there are no "right" answers to these questions. Here are some tips for when you feel "stuck" or "draw a blank" with an exercise:

- Just make up an answer. Whatever you write will turn out to be just what you need to say.

- Answer the question, "Suppose you did know; then what would you write?"

- What would _____ [someone who knows you well] say about how you would answer?

Using these prompts can help you bypass the resistance you may have to doing the exercises.

Evaluating the Impact of the Exercises

To assess the impact of how a particular exercise affects your mood, you'll be asked to rate your mood before and after the exercise, using a ten-point scale, with 1 meaning "totally miserable" and 10 meaning "good." Different people experience depression differently. Some people feel it more in their thoughts, having thoughts of doom and hopelessness. Some experience depression more emotionally; they feel sad and cry. Others experience depression in a physical way. They may have queasiness, headaches, fatigue, chest tension, or a knot in the stomach. Others experience a combination of these symptoms. Considering all your symptoms together, rate your mood before you do the activity and then afterward to determine the effect of the exercise on your mood.

One reason for rating your moods is to make concrete and quantifiable what's sometimes experienced as amorphous and overwhelming. When you capture your level of depression with a number, it becomes much more manageable. Another reason to track your moods is that depression makes it difficult for you to see any small shifts in mood. This is partly due to the irrationality of depression. It colors how you experience everything: people seem unreliable, the past is painful, and the future is hopeless. You'll probably find this hard to believe at this point, but this isn't necessarily the reality of your situation. By making a numerical assessment of your feelings before and after doing the exercises, you'll take note of how completing the exercises has been helpful and in what ways. By writing down what you've learned, you can solidify the lesson.

Although I predict there'll be at least small, positive shifts in mood as a result of the exercises, you could also feel sadness at certain realizations. For example, Peter felt sad after doing a particular exercise that asked him to identify his role models, because he became aware that he had none. On the other hand, when asked to find a role model, he felt more hopeful that he could gain some guidance for his life.

Coping

This section will get you to think about how you've dealt with your depression. In other words, what do you do and say that helps you keep going? Some of your methods may be healthy ways of coping, and some may be unhealthy. Don't ignore the unhealthy coping questions (you'll find more on these in chapter 6). Sometimes it's hard to know what's an unhealthy coping method and what's a positive one. Some activities are fine to do sometimes, such as watching TV, working, sleeping, reading trashy novels, or searching the Internet. Indeed, "distraction" can be a healthy coping method. Here are some guidelines for when a coping method may be unhealthy:

- You do these activities exclusively or obsessively.

- You do these activities to avoid your problems.

- You ignore your duties or relationships.

- Other people complain about the behavior.

- These activities cause impairment, for example, unhealthy weight gain when you overeat as a way of coping.

For now, you'll look at your positive, or at least harmless, ways of managing your depression. At this point you might react this way: "I'm not dealing with my depression; otherwise, why would I feel so bad?" You probably aren't noticing or giving yourself credit for even the small efforts you make toward helping yourself positively influence your mood. A magnified focus on these efforts will help you realize what's helpful and how you can amplify the steps you take to pull out of your depression.

■ *Case Examples*

To begin, I'll introduce a few examples, so you can see how others have coped with their depression. You may also find yourself identifying with some of these examples, and getting ideas for how to manage your symptoms, as well.

Debra: *Debra, who's fifty, says that her relationships with her family members keep her going. She knows they depend on her and feels committed to always being there for them, no matter how bad she feels at times. When considering her qualities that contribute to this commitment, she decides that this means she's a person who cares about other people. She doesn't want to hurt the people she loves, so she wants to be there for them.*

Samantha: *Samantha, who's forty-five, answers that her three dogs keep her going. They're a reason to get up in the morning. She has to take them out for walks twice a day, and they accompany her in the car when she drives to do errands. Samantha chose these dogs because they were kind of "funny looking" and she didn't think anybody else would adopt them from the animal shelter. She's proud that she was able to give them a "second chance," and realizes that without her intervention, they would've been euthanized. In a small way, this fact gives her life meaning: that she was able to save their lives and that her day is now structured around taking care of them in other ways. The dogs also give her affection and attention, and lick her tears away if she feels really bad on a particular day and cries. The fact that she takes such good care of her dogs means that she's a good person who cares about living beings.*

Ellen: *A seventy-eight-year-old woman with chronic obstructive pulmonary disease, Ellen is connected to an oxygen machine at all times, which hinders her mobility. Additionally, she recently fell and had to have hip surgery. Her eyesight has also deteriorated, and she has difficulty reading, an activity she used to enjoy. As a result, she feels trapped in her apartment and "cut off from the world." Ellen enjoys watching the news and listening to radio talk shows to stay current with politics, which has been a lifetime passion. She states that the TV is a good distraction and she enjoys watching political news shows. She also forces herself to get outside every day for some fresh air. She describes herself as strong willed and stubborn at times, and believes that that's what other people would say keeps her going.*

Hanna: *Hanna, a thirty-eight-year-old woman who emigrated from Ethiopia ten years ago, has recently left her husband, who physically abused her during their marriage. Hanna's husband used to tell her that if she left him, she wouldn't be able to make it on her own and could never make enough money to provide for the children without him. He predicted that she would eventually take her own life. Some of the time since the divorce, Hanna's been scared that he was right, but about 30 percent of the time, she feels angry. Hanna reports that this anger has made her stronger, strengthening her resolve to survive and thrive.*

In response to the question, "What would others say keeps you going?" Hanna writes, "What Americans would say is very different from what Ethiopians would say. Ethiopians would say that I'm stupid for leaving my husband, because he makes much money. Ethiopian women would tell me that a husband has the right to beat his wife, and that a good wife will accept such beatings and learn not to anger her husband. Ethiopian women would tell me that a woman doesn't leave a husband because he sleeps with other women. But American women would tell me that I'm right to flee a husband who abuses me and that children are abused by witnessing domestic violence. Americans would tell me that being safe and free is better than staying with a bad husband."

Hanna further writes in response to the coping questions, "When I feel sad, I try to have hope that things will get better, because I believe in the Bible and have faith that something good will happen, that something good will follow." Hanna stated that her spiritual belief has kept her from giving up, and provides the courage and hope to make a new life for herself and her children.

Rate your mood. Now, to get started, before you begin the opening exercise, rate your mood on a scale from 1 to 10: _____ .

EXERCISE: Explore Your Hidden Resources

To get in touch with your hidden resources for dealing with your depression, think back to a time when you felt very sad but still had to meet a commitment, such as going to work, getting your children off to school, or doing something you'd promised to do. This exercise, as well as the one that follows, focuses on your positive coping methods; however, if negative coping methods come up, such as drinking, using drugs, overeating, or excessive TV watching, jot these down under question 9. You'll note that there's not a sample response for every aspect of coping. The reason is that, although many different resources are potentially available to you, like many people, you're drawing on only a few. This exercise will help you get in touch with what coping methods you're using, as well as other areas you could potentially tap into.

1. Write down what you said to yourself that enabled you to get out of your sadness temporarily in order to meet that commitment. *Example:* Every morning, Nicole felt overwhelmed by the amount of work it took to get herself out of bed to get her children ready on time for school. But even though it was hard, she did it every day. When she stopped to think about what got her up and active in the mornings, she realized that she often gave herself the following "pep talk" when she felt she absolutely couldn't do it: "It'll be a lot of work now, but once they're in school, I'll have some time to myself. I can do this. I've done it many mornings, and I can do it now."

_____

_____

_____

_____

2. In this situation, what were the actions you took? *Example:* Nicole started by saying, "Okay, kids, let's have some cereal and milk. You can sit at the table and finish while I make your lunches. Once you do that, I'll help you get dressed, and Mommy will get dressed too. So I'll really need your help, and then we'll be out of here in no time." By breaking it down for them, it didn't sound as overwhelming to her.

_____

_____

_____

_____

3. What kind of help did you seek in this situation?

_____

_____

_____

_____

4.   What financial or other types of physical resources did you draw upon to get through?

_____

_____

_____

_____

5.   What spiritual resources did you draw upon to help with this situation? *Example:* Nicole said she prayed to God for guidance to get through the morning. She said this made her feel that she wasn't so alone and that someone was rooting for her.

_____

_____

_____

_____

6.   What personal qualities did you draw upon in this situation? *Example:* Nicole called upon her sense of responsibility (she liked to be on time for events) and her caring for her children (she wanted to be a good mother) to get her through this situation.

_____

_____

_____

_____

7.   What would others say you do? *Example:* At first, Nicole said, "No one knows what I go through. They see me dropping my kids off at school, and I'm sure they think I'm just like everyone else." Upon further reflection, she realized that she looked as together as any of the other mothers and that there were other parents who were sometimes late, like her.

_____

_____

_____

_____

8. Summarize here what you've learned about your coping resources. *Example:* Nicole has identified a number of things that allow her to keep going: (a) she cares about her children and wants the best for them, (b) she uses her spirituality to cope with situations that overwhelm her, and (c) she uses her thoughts to help her get through a difficult situation, such as, "It'll take a lot of work now, but it'll soon be over and then I'll have time for myself."

_____

_____

_____

_____

9. What negative coping methods do you realize you rely upon? (We'll deal with these in chapter 6.) *Example:* Nicole stayed in bed too long, unwilling to face the day. As a result, she had even less time to get ready in the morning. She also found herself shouting at the children as they dawdled.

_____

_____

_____

_____

10. Now, you'll explore the resources that are potentially available to you.

    a. Write down what you could've said to yourself to make the situation more manageable. *Example:* Nicole could tell herself, "Everyone has to go through this with children. This is the way children act. They dawdle because they find other activities more interesting than getting ready. It's not that my children are bad or are purposefully doing this to get on my nerves."

    _____

    _____

    _____

b.   In this situation, what were the actions you could've taken? *Example:* Nicole could have gotten out of bed on time or set her alarm earlier. She also could have turned off the television so that the children focused on getting ready rather than watching programs.

_____

_____

_____

c.   What kind of help could you seek in this situation? *Examples:* (1) Nicole could say to her husband, "I need more help in the morning in getting the kids ready for school. Could you get their breakfast and make their lunches, and I'll get them dressed and brush their hair?" (2) Nicole could make arrangements with another parent who lives nearby to trade off mornings: "One day I'll take your kids to school, and the next day, you can take mine." (3) Nicole could solicit help from her children: "From now on, I'm going to need more help from you to get you to school on time. This is the schedule I've written down for us each morning to follow, and I'm going to paste it up on the wall. You guys will get an extra TV show in the afternoon when you come home from school if you can follow the schedule in the morning and get along with each other." (4) Nicole could hire a neighborhood preteen to act as a "mother's helper" to assist with the morning schedule. (5) If she has a mother, mother-in-law, or other close relative who lives in the area, she could ask her to come over and help her in the morning.

_____

_____

_____

d.   What financial or other types of physical resources could you draw upon to get through? *Example:* If Nicole hired a "mother's helper," she could use household money to pay for this kind of help.

_____

_____

_____

e.   What spiritual resources could you draw upon to help with this situation? *Example:* Nicole said that when she felt that she was starting to "lose it" with her children, she could take a "time-out" and pray so that she could feel more equipped to deal with the situation.

_____

_____

_____

f.   What personal qualities could you draw upon in this situation? *Example:* Nicole could draw on her creativity to devise a way to make a game of getting ready for her children or to reward the child who got ready first with a piece of candy.

_____

_____

_____

How Did This Exercise Help?

Rate on a scale from 1 to 10 (in which 10 means "fine") how you feel now: _____ . How does this number differ from your initial rating? How do you account for any changes?

_____

_____

_____

_____

You probably discovered that you have more resources than you initially believed you had. By working with a specific example like this, you can start to examine how you make yourself feel better. People often experience depression in a way that feels overwhelming. When you start to look at specific situations that get you down, you may start to realize that "depression" is made up of certain incidents that can be broken down and worked on. Through this exercise, you may also see that you're actively engaged in a process to help yourself, despite how you feel. You're perhaps more competent than how you saw yourself before. By learning that there are even more coping resources available, you may feel more hopeful about your ability to cope.

EXERCISE: Find Your Strengths, Even at a Low Point

Before you begin the next exercise, note that it may or may not apply to you. If you haven't had this experience, feel free to skip it and move ahead. If you do find it applicable, rate your mood on a scale from 1 to 10 here: _____ .

Did you ever think that life wasn't worth living and that you'd rather not be around? If you've had such an experience, consider the following questions:

1. What did you say to yourself at that time that kept you from harming yourself? *Example:* Samantha has said to herself, "I can't do anything to hurt myself, because my mother would be devastated. Plus, I have my dogs to take care of. What would happen to them?"

_____

_____

_____

_____

2. What actions did you take? *Example:* Samantha called a supportive friend. When he wasn't home, she called another friend she could talk to, and explored how she felt. Crying and talking about her feelings, she said, relieved some of the "blackness" in her head. Most important, when she talked about feeling suicidal, her friend told her that she mattered to him and that it would have a big impact on him if she died.

_____

_____

_____

_____

3. What spiritual resources did you draw upon? *Example:* Samantha drew on her spiritual beliefs that suicide was a sin and that she would end up in hell if she did anything to herself.

_____

_____

_____

_____

4. What supports did you draw upon? *Example:* Samantha drew heavily on the support of her friends. Note that she had more than one friend she could call when she felt this amount of pain.

_____

_____

_____

_____

5. What financial or other physical resources did you draw upon? *Example:* Samantha had a car, so she could take a drive when she felt "the walls closing in on" her.

_____

_____

_____

_____

6. What personal qualities did you use in this situation? *Example:* Samantha drew on the love and caring she had for her mother and her pets.

_____

_____

_____

_____

7. What would others say you do? *Example:* Samantha had been told by one of her employers that she was "resourceful." Samantha said she'd been surprised by this observation because she'd never really thought of herself this way, but she decided that it was also true of how she handled her depression. She would call her friends, and was good about reaching out for help. Because she didn't want to be a burden and didn't want her relationships to be only "one-way," she reciprocated by being available for them when they wanted to talk.

_____

_____

_____

_____

8. Summarize here what you've learned about your coping resources. *Example:* Samantha said that her involvement with her dogs and other people kept her going. She felt blessed that she had friends she could reach out to when she felt really bad. Also, she had spiritual beliefs that prohibited suicide. Plus, owning a car meant that she had the freedom to leave her apartment and go places.

_____

_____

_____

_____

9. What other coping methods are potentially available to you?

   a. Write down what you could've said to yourself to make the situation more manageable. *Example:* Samantha could say, "I've gone through these bad periods before, but yet I've always gotten through them. This will pass too, even though it doesn't feel like it."

   _____

   _____

   _____

   b. In this situation, what were the actions you could've taken? *Example:* Samantha could take her dogs for a long walk. That way, she would give herself meaning by giving them some pleasure. It would also give her fresh air and exercise, which might help her feel better.

   _____

   _____

   _____

c. What kind of help could you seek in this situation? *Example:* Samantha could call a therapist and make an appointment to discuss her thoughts of self-harm.

_____

_____

_____

d. What financial or other types of physical resources could you draw upon to get through? *Example:* Samantha had health insurance with her job and an employee-assistance program, so she had the resources to seek psychological help.

_____

_____

_____

e. What spiritual resources could you draw upon to help with this situation? *Example:* Samantha said that writing a prayer might help. Since the thoughts in her head were so bad, writing something down might help to overcome these thoughts and replace them with another perspective.

_____

_____

_____

f. What personal qualities could you draw upon in this situation? *Example:* Rather than see herself as "weak" and "powerless" when she was in these moods, Samantha considered that she might actually be a "survivor" for being able to make it through these difficult periods.

_____

_____

_____

10. What negative coping methods do you realize you rely upon? (These will be dealt with in chapter 6.) *Example:* Samantha said that instead of eating a regular meal when she felt bad, she would eat sweet foods like ice cream and cake to comfort herself.

_____

_____

_____

_____

How Did This Exercise Help?

Rate your mood now on a scale from 1 to 10 (in which 10 means "fine"): _____ . How does this number differ from your initial rating? How do you account for any changes you made?

_____

_____

_____

_____

Finding Meaning

In this section, you'll address a symptom that lies at the heart of depression, the sense of meaninglessness that often pervades the experience. People who experience meaninglessness usually express it in the following ways: "Why am I alive?" and "What's the point?" Nothing seems to matter or have any purpose.

Before you explore this topic, I suggest assessing the impact of this work with a slightly different scale from the ones you've used before. This time, on a scale from 1 to 10, assess your sense that your life has meaning in a global way, in which 10 means "very meaningful." Put your rating here: _____ .

I know that depression is very painful, and if you had a choice, you'd likely elect to rid yourself of it. But since you're depressed right now, can you see any good that has come out of it? In other words, is there any "silver lining"? This might be a hard question, so think more specifically about different areas of your life: What personal strengths have you developed?

What opportunities have come your way? Have you forged new or deeper relationships as a result of dealing with depression? A lot of research has shown that when people can find benefits after a major stressor, they feel better and aren't as depressed as people who can't do so (Helgeson, Reynolds, and Tomich 2006).

You might be stumped by this question, but the following examples might help you see this differently or help you come up with other ideas.

■ *Case Examples*

Nicole: *Nicole wrote that her depression has helped her feel compassion for other people who suffer from pain. This compassion drew her to volunteer at a hospice organization, because she felt she could understand those who were facing extreme physical pain or family members who were grieving the loss of a loved one.*

Debra: *Debra said that being depressed helped her get a lot done. When she felt depressed, she liked to write a list and cross things off as she did them. This made her feel as if her day had some meaning, that she had at least accomplished something, no matter how depressed she felt.*

Monique: *Monique said that she has deepened the relationships with other people in her life by confiding in them about how she feels during her down times. Because she had confided in them, her friends, in turn, started being "real" with her, and their relationships are stronger and deeper than they might've been otherwise.*

Some people believe that a sense of meaning and purpose is either there or it's not. However, at times you have to work to make meaning out of an event or an experience. You may be able to find meaning in your depression if you notice that it gives you more understanding about yourself and other people, empathy toward the suffering of others, or closer relationships to others. Other people may find religious or spiritual meaning in their struggles with depression, seeing the experience as an ordeal meant to make them stronger or a suffering that's a part of life experience. For example, Simone talked to her therapist about "meaninglessness." When the therapist asked about her spiritual beliefs, Simone said that the religion of her upbringing left her "cold" and didn't provide any sense of meaning. However, the therapist helped Simone reframe her sense of meaninglessness by suggesting that this feeling of seeking and thirsting for a sense of meaning might point to the fact that Simone is a spiritual person who hasn't yet found a spiritual practice that provides meaning, rather than that Simone's life is inherently meaningless. This helped Simone recast her symptom in a different light, as a searching process (rather than the "blanket grayness" that she'd experienced previously) that meant that she was a spiritual person, rather than a bad person for not following the religious teachings of her upbringing.

EXERCISE: Find Meaning in Depression

What meaning can you make out of your experience of depression?

_____

_____

_____

_____

Having finished reading this material, rate your sense of the "meaningfulness" of your life from 1 to 10: _____ . How does this number differ from your initial rating? What do you think caused any change?

_____

_____

_____

_____

PUTTING IT ALL TOGETHER: A PLAN FOR COPING

This chapter has been about the different ways you manage your depressive symptoms. Based on what you've learned from the material in this chapter, including what you've written down and the ideas you've gained from the examples, pull together your own unique coping plan. Consider this your "emergency plan" for when depression hits. You can either write it down here and tear it out to keep in a desk drawer or tape onto the fridge, or you can prepare a smaller version that's separate from this book so that you can carry it with you. The reason to have a written reminder nearby is that in the midst of depression, it's often difficult to keep from getting overwhelmed by the feelings. When you see that you have a concrete plan to deal with the specific situation you're facing, the magnitude of the depression is reduced, and you become more empowered about your ability to cope.

Consider the following elements for your plan:

Actions: What can you do?

_____

_____

_____

_____

Thoughts: What can you say to yourself?

_____

_____

_____

_____

Support: Whom can you reach out to?

_____

_____

_____

_____

Finances: What financial and other physical resources can you draw upon?

_____

_____

_____

_____

Spirituality: What spiritual resources can you draw upon?

_____

_____

_____

_____

Personal Qualities: What qualities can you draw upon?

_____

_____

_____

_____

Relationship Questions: What do the important people in your life say you can do the next time you feel depressed?

_____

_____

_____

_____

CONCLUSION

This chapter has been about validating your struggle with depression. The exercises in this chapter have been designed so that you can reflect on the ways in which you have the strength to keep going. By exploring the various domains of your life—what you say to yourself, your actions, your personal qualities, the supports you use—you may find that your perspective has changed. Answering the questions in this chapter has shown your resourcefulness in making efforts to resolve the way you feel, and that there's some meaning to the experience of depression and your life. This chapter has helped you start the process of identifying these resources—and also amplifying them so that you can use them more intentionally in overcoming your depression. You'll continue this process in the next chapter.

CHAPTER 2

Cultivating Resilience

Resilience is the ability to do well in life despite stressful circumstances. People who show resilience have certain ways of approaching hardship, as well as particular personality traits (such as confidence) and environmental supports (such as family and friends) that help them face difficult situations and come through all right. Resilience is made up of the interplay between risk and protective factors. *Risk factors* are situations that exist in the individual (such as a genetic vulnerability toward depression) or the environment (stressful life events) that make it more likely that problems like depression will occur. *Protective factors* counterbalance risk factors in that they involve individual factors (such as intelligence) or environmental factors (such as social support) that decrease the likelihood that a problem like depression will develop. Risk and protective factors work together to determine whether a disorder will develop and, if one does occur, the likelihood of recovery.

In this chapter, I present the risk and protective factors that have been established for recovery from depression. Then you'll explore various domains of your life, and see how you can bolster your identified protective factors and mitigate some of your risk factors for depression. For example, you might show certain strengths in your work settings (such as good time management, people skills, organizational skills, assertiveness, or problem-solving abilities) or hobbies (such as creativity, physical agility, or persistence) but may have lost touch with them, feeling instead that you just don't have what it takes to be successful or happy. The material and exercises in this chapter will help you:

- Feel better

- Pinpoint the areas of your life and aspects of yourself that you can call upon to vanquish depression

- Discover solutions that you can apply to problem situations

---

RISK AND PROTECTIVE FACTORS FOR DEPRESSION

Research has identified the risk factors associated with depression. A genetic predisposition toward this disorder explains a lot about why people get depressed, but it's not the whole picture (Sullivan, Neale, and Kendler 2000). Stressful life events, such as abuse and loss, also contribute a great deal to the development of depression (Bonomi et al. 2008). Individual ways of responding to and coping with life events also enter the picture. For instance, if you ruminate, that is, endlessly think about problems without coming to any resolution, this type of coping style is associated with depression (Nolen-Hoeksema 2002). However, an active problem-solving style helps mitigate depression and is, thus, a protective factor. Having supportive people in their lives also helps people prevent depression (Kraaij, Arensman, and Spinhoven 2002).

Once depression has occurred, risk and protective factors for the individual's propensity to recover from the episode and to prevent further depressive episodes cluster into the following areas (Meyers et al. 2002; Bockting et al. 2006; and Mueller et al. 1999):

- Features of the depression

- Biological aspects

- Psychological aspects

- Social aspects

Features of Depression

There are certain *features of depression* that point toward an earlier recovery:

- A later-in-life onset (after young adulthood)

- Having fewer symptoms of depression (which were named in chapter 1)

- Being depressed for a shorter period of time

That last factor is why it's important to address depression when it hits, so that it doesn't get worse.

Biological Factors

At the *biological level*, good health—in terms of being free from a chronic disease, such as heart disease, multiple sclerosis, HIV, and so forth—promotes recovery from depression.

Psychological Factors

Psychologically, if you don't have any other mental health disorders, such as substance abuse, eating disorders, or anxiety, it's easier to recover from depression, because you only have to struggle against one problem and there's no other disorder to handicap your efforts to move forward. A sense of hope also bolsters recovery. Since I recognize that hopelessness is a core symptom of depression, I'll help you build a sense of hope in chapter 3. Finally, a way of handling life challenges that's oriented toward action and finding solutions is more adaptive for recovery than avoiding your problems or ruminating. In chapter 1, the process of doing the exercises helped you get in touch with the many coping methods you have at your disposal, and developing active, problem-focused coping strategies will be a continuing focus of this workbook.

Social Factors

At the *social level*, family support is important. Chapter 9 will address communication skills, to help you gain more support and ease any possible conflict that might get in the way of your recovery. Social support, which means having close friends you can confide in (just one or two people is fine) and family members behind you, also helps considerably. This workbook discusses a lot about how to increase your social support, because it's such a critical component of recovery (and prevention of new episodes of depression). Additionally, if stressful life events (romantic breakups, moves, job loss, and so forth) are at a minimum, it's easier to get better. Finally, people who are comfortable financially tend to recover more easily from depression than people who are poor, because those living in poverty suffer more stress and have fewer resources to get appropriate help.

In the following section, you'll be asked to take inventory of your risk and protective factors so that you can decrease any risk factors (such as rumination) and increase protective factors (the use of positive coping methods). Although there are certain things you can't do anything about, such as your genes, there are plenty of other aspects you do have control over.

■ *Case Example: Tammy*

Here I'll return to the example of Tammy in chapter 1. In looking at her circumstances, I've categorized her risk and protective factors in the following ways:

RISK AND PROTECTIVE FACTORS FOR TAMMY'S RECOVERY FROM DEPRESSION

	Risk Factors	Protective Factors
Features of Depression:		• Has had no prior episodes of depression • Despite having major depression, meets minimal criteria
Biological Factors:	• Has a serious and chronic health problem	
Psychological Factors:	• Smokes marijuana often when she feels down	• Is grateful for what she has • Has strong religious faith • Believes she can get through her difficult circumstances (has hope)
Social Factors:	• Poor social support • A difficult housing situation • Poverty	• Takes advantage of services for her disability at the rehabilitation hospital

When you first read about Tammy, you may have been struck by how difficult her life sounded. However, when laying out the risk factors (five total) and protective factors (six total), you can see that the protective side of the equation is slightly higher. Although she faces many challenges, she has a lot going for her in the protective column. Additionally, she can work with or get help for some of the risk factors to reduce them. Although she can't change the fact that she has multiple sclerosis, she can control how she manages her illness. Further, she can change her ways of coping with her life stressors and develop better social support. Finally, there are other, more formal support services she can access, such as a support group for people with MS and nonprofit legal assistance to help her get out of debt.

Rate your mood. Before beginning the following exercise, rate your mood here on a scale from 1 to 10: _____ .

EXERCISE: Explore Your Risk and Protective Factors

Following are tables for you to fill in: one for risk factors and one for protective factors. Write down your responses (yes or no).

RISK FACTORS FOR YOUR RECOVERY FROM DEPRESSION

	Risk Influences	Yes or No
Features of Depression:	• More symptoms of depression • Prior depressive episodes • Presence of residual symptoms (after the depressive episode is over, you still feel some symptoms) • Depression came on early in your life (childhood or adolescence)	
Biological Factors:	• Medical conditions or poor general health	
Psychological Factors:	• Other mental health disorders	
Social Factors:	• Weak family relationships • Being unmarried • Stressful life events • Low socioeconomic status	

PROTECTIVE FACTORS FOR YOUR RECOVERY FROM DEPRESSION

	Protective Influences	Yes or No
Features of the Depression:	• Lower levels of depression • No prior episodes • No residual symptoms • Onset later in life • Early assessment	
Biological Factors:	• Good health	
Psychological Factors:	• Lack of coexisting disorder	
Social Factors:	• Strong family relations and social support • Middle-to-high socioeconomic status	

Count up the risk factors you've indicated and then the number of protective factors. Which category has more responses? Unfortunately, many of the risk factors can't be changed, but no matter what your risk factor, you can still control how you react to these events and cope with them. One of the themes of this workbook is how you can use your many resources to cope with your depression and other stressful events.

How Did This Exercise Help?

Returning to the 1 to 10 scale, rate how you feel now: _____ . What do you think has caused the difference in how you felt before the exercise and how you feel now?

_____

_____

_____

_____

FINDING RESILIENCE IN OTHER AREAS OF YOUR LIFE

In this section of the chapter, you'll examine other areas of your life outside your depression to find the potential resources within and around you. These will be areas of your life related to the risk and protective factors I've named. For instance, *social support* is a key protective factor. *Good coping methods* include hobbies, interests, and spirituality. *Stressful life events* are risk factors for depression, so you'll be asked about how you handled any past abuse and crisis situations. Finally, you'll explore your *parenting, caretaking,* and *employment* experiences for additional resources you may currently be unaware of. Bob Bertolino and Bill O'Hanlon (2002) have come up with some excellent strengths-based assessment questions in *Collaborative, Competency-Based Counseling and Therapy* that I've adapted with permission for a self-help format.

Informal Social Support

Research has repeatedly shown the importance of a support network in preventing the development of depression, and in helping people cope and recover from depression if it does occur. When you have people you can turn to for emotional support and companionship, this can create meaning in your life and make a big difference in how you feel. Some people say that they have a strong support network, but no one in it really knows how they feel. Reyna, a second-generation young woman from Iran, said that she was close to her family but that they didn't know how bad she felt because she didn't "want them to worry."

Many depressed people aren't good at asking for help from others. (For more work on feeling undeserving of help, chapter 8 will work extensively on such beliefs that feed into depression.) As an example, Moira, a thirty-two-year-old woman, complained that she received no help from her husband or her relatives (whom she'd helped in the past) in taking care of her children and managing her household. However, she also revealed that she'd never asked for help. Her response was, "They should know. They see me struggling and should just pitch in. That's what I'd do for someone." If you can relate to Moira's situation, you'll learn more in chapter 9 about how to reach out to others in a way that helps you get what you need.

As another example, Peter realizes that he has difficulty asking for help, but also knows that he and his wife talked a lot when they were first married, especially about issues that came up from differences in their socioeconomic backgrounds. Peter can draw on the fact that he was able to communicate with his wife about tough subjects in the past. This helps him know that he can also talk to her about a difficult subject for him now, such as how he feels when he's depressed. He also appreciates how supportive his wife is of him, and knows that she wants him to feel better. This signals to him that she might be available to him at times when he feels his worst.

People with depression have a tendency to socially isolate. The problem with withdrawal from social contact is that you don't get a chance to experience possible company, understanding and shared experience, enjoyment, and the fun that being with others can bring. I brought up cognitive behavioral therapy in the introduction to this book. According to this type of therapy, the main reason depression arises is lack of reinforcement from the environment. Social contacts can provide a lot of reinforcement. Another problem with social withdrawal is that negative thinking can spiral downward without the reality check that others can provide: "No one likes me." "I'm all alone in the world." "No one would miss me if I were gone." Further, social isolation can breed negative ways of coping. People tend not to overeat or excessively watch television as much when they're with others as when they're alone.

The following examples show how other people who struggled with depression called upon the support they had available to them.

■ *Case Examples*

Peter: *Peter, a twenty-eight-year-old army enlistee who's been deployed to Iraq three times, identified his wife as the person he's closest to. He said, "My wife really listens to me and tries to understand where I'm coming from, no matter how uncommunicative I can be. She really pushes me to get support and worries about me. She and her daughter from a previous relationship have made the most difference in my life. My daughter saved me, because when she was born, I was in a bad place—doing drugs—and would've ended up either dead or in jail. I quit because she was important to me. My wife has also made a positive difference. She constantly strives to help me be a better person and broaden my views." Peter admitted that he didn't like asking for help. "Ever since I can remember, I've been dealing with the depression on my own. It was only recently that I received help through the army. This was only because of my PTSD (post-traumatic stress disorder) diagnosis. I guess, if I needed help I could ask my wife." Asked about his heroes, Peter answered, "This question makes me very sad. I realize that I don't have any heroes. I've never really looked up to anyone or had any real positive role models in my life to strive to be like."*

Hilary: *Hilary, who is forty-five, suffers from bipolar disorder, and finds the depressive parts of her illness the hardest to handle, said that her father has been a tremendous help to her. When she's in a depressive episode, he flies to her city and stays with her until the "worst is over." He even drives her around, and they go places together, even if it's only simple activities like grocery shopping.*

Hanna: *Hanna stated that, other than her children and her remaining family in Ethiopia, she's closest to her best American friend, Janice. Hanna said, "Although she is a woman, she has helped me and my children more than my husband ever did. I can count on her to be there for me and for my children." Hanna also talked about her oldest brother, who convinced her father that a woman should be educated, and helped pay for her university training.*

Sarah: *Sarah, seventy-five, said her grandmother, a teacher, made the most positive differ-ence in her life. Sarah's grandmother had an abusive husband and divorced him in a time when divorces weren't socially accepted. She also got her degree and became a teacher. Sarah said she looked up to her grandmother for all the strengths she had. Sarah became a teacher herself because of her grandmother's positive influence.*

Rate your mood. Rate your mood here on a scale from 1 to 10: _____.

EXERCISE: Explore Your Informal Social Support

Reflect on the following questions about your social support that have been adapted from Bertolino and O'Hanlon (2002, 77):

1. When have others helped you? Think about a recent situation, or one that stands out in your mind, in which you received help from someone when you felt depressed or were struggling with another problem. What did that person do that helped? How did you let that person know that you needed help?

_____

_____

_____

_____

2. For each person you're close to, what drew that person to you (depending on that person's relationship to you: friend, spouse, parent, child, grandparent, colleague, and so on)? Recall how you met and how you became closer. You might not actually know the *real* answer to this question, but you can think hypothetically if you don't feel comfortable asking the person at this time. If you did know, what do you think that person would say?

Person #1's name and possible response:

_____

_____

Person #2's name and possible response:

_____

_____

Person #3's name and possible response:

_____

_____

3. If you have a romantic partner, how were you able to attract that person to you? What qualities and behaviors did your partner see in you that made him or her want to be with you? You might not really know what your partner thinks, but you can always ask. If you'd rather not, you can reflect on this question hypothetically. If you have the impulse to respond in a cynical way (for example, "She's only with me because I give her money"), try to find the positive side of this reason (examples: "I'm generous" or "I'm a good financial provider"). If you can't reframe your answer in this way, the relationship might be one you'd like to explore further in chapter 6.

_____

_____

_____

_____

4. Which relationships have challenged you? How did you manage them?

_____

_____

_____

_____

How Did This Exercise Help?

Having completed this exercise, rate your mood here on a scale from 1 to 10: _____ . How does this number differ from your initial rating? What do you think has caused the change?

_____

_____

_____

_____

Formal Social Support

The previous section centered on informal social support, from family and friends. Now you'll turn to any formal support system with which you're involved currently or you were in the past. Formal social support includes self-help groups, psychotherapists, doctors, and other helping resources. It's fine whether you're seeking professional help at this time or not, because this workbook can be used either for self-help or along with professional treatment. (If this section doesn't apply to you, feel free to skip to the next section.)

Many people believe that seeking help from services is a sign of weakness, that they can't handle their problems by themselves and should be able to. They may also view seeking outside help as an admission that they're "crazy." On the contrary, seeking help may indicate an enormous amount of courage. It shows that you're willing to admit that you need help, to become vulnerable with a person you don't know, and to possibly delve into subjects or discussions that are painful for you. But even if you do seek outside support, you remain the expert on yourself; you're an active participant in any process of help-seeking to make it work for you (Bertolino and O'Hanlon 2002).

The following examples show how inquiry into prior help-seeking leads people to feel more empowered about their efforts to help themselves.

■ *Case Examples*

Estelle: *Estelle, twenty-seven, says that the most invaluable part of therapy was learning that when she feels suicidal, she's actually angry. Recognizing this and learning how to express herself assertively during conflict stopped her from feeling suicidal.*

Peter: *Peter has received both individual and group therapy for his PTSD and depression, but he says, "Group has been most helpful, because I know I'm not alone. It's good to know that the person next to you feels just like you do and that everyone's working through their issues together. There's something healing in knowing that you're not the only one experiencing a problem. I also realized I can offer my experiences and feelings to my group members, and that helps them, too."*

Peter said he didn't find the individual therapy helpful at all; he didn't connect with the therapist and felt that his therapist was inexperienced. He also mentioned that he'd been on a couple of different medications. "I was first put on one, and I hated it. It made my depression worse. I then switched, and the new drug helped me suppress some of the bad feelings and thoughts I normally have." Peter said the medication helped him live. "I was both suicidal and homicidal before the medication. Now I'm doing much better. I was able to get my life back—not completely but a lot better than before."

Sarah: *Sarah's a seventy-five-year-old woman whose husband recently died of colon cancer. She states that the bereavement services she receives from hospice are helpful, because they provide her with company since she doesn't like to be alone. Additionally, the education on grief and the bereavement process has assisted her in learning that the emotions she's experiencing are normal and that she's "not going crazy." She said that hospice was most beneficial, because staff were present at her house when her husband died, even though it was the middle of the night.*

Rob: *Rob said he didn't like it when his therapist "got on me about my drinking." He said, "She kept talking about it on and on, and I honestly didn't know why, but when I tried to stop, just to prove her wrong, I found out that it wasn't so easy. That was when I realized I did need to get a handle on my drinking. I'm not an alcoholic or anything, but I was wasting a lot of time drinking in the evenings when I felt lonely."*

Nicole: *Nicole answered that the antidepressant medication had helped her sleep and that this was worth "its weight in gold," because she'd suffered from chronic insomnia. "Just knowing that I'm going to get a good night's sleep makes me feel better, because I don't have to worry about lying awake at night. That's when I used to feel my worst."*

Snyder: *Snyder's a fifty-four-year-old man whose job was recently phased out, and he was having some difficulty finding another one. Snyder said that, while antidepressant medication hadn't affected his depression per se, he noticed that he had less anxiety when speaking in front of other people. The medication helped him "keep my cool," and he was more liable to seek out social situations than he had in the past, because he felt a great sense of confidence. In turn, acting confidently in social situations helped him feel better about himself, and being more social helped lift the depression. Snyder said that, although the medication had helped reduce his anxiety, he was the one who still had to take the risk in approaching people and trying to find ways to connect with them.*

Rate your mood. Rate your mood here on a scale from 1 to 10: _____ .

EXERCISE: Explore Your Formal Social Support

The questions in this exercise have been adapted from *Collaborative, Competency-Based Counseling and Therapy*, by Bob Bertolino and Bill O'Hanlon (2002, 77).

1. What circumstances, situations, or feelings made you decide to get treatment?

_____

_____

_____

_____

2. What have you found helpful about any professional treatment you've received?

_____

_____

_____

_____

3. What did you find least helpful about the treatment experience?

_____

_____

_____

_____

4. If you're currently on medication for depression or another mental health issue, or if you were previously, how did it assist you?

_____

_____

_____

_____

How Did This Exercise Help?

Having completed this exercise, rate your mood here on a scale from 1 to 10: _____ .
How does this number differ from your initial rating, and what do you think made the difference?

_____

_____

_____

_____

Hobbies, Interests, and Activities

You may wonder why you're being asked about hobbies and interests, and how it fits in with talking about exploring your strengths. Here are a couple of reasons: First, if you're depressed, it's important to do something pleasurable (and hopefully more than one thing) every day, which can make you feel better (Clarke and Lewinsohn 1995). Being absorbed in an activity can get your mind off how you feel. Distraction can be a helpful way to prevent depression from taking hold. The other reason to explore hobbies and interests is that this may be an area in your life where you show certain strengths. By identifying these strengths, you can get in touch with more of your positive attributes. Therefore, this section is about finding both activities that will help you, and the resources and strengths that underlie these activities.

■ *Case Examples*

Peter: *Peter writes that he's part of a soccer team with his army friends. Although he's injured now, he still goes to the games. He can still play golf and does so at least a couple of times a week with his friends. He inevitably feels better when he knows he has games scheduled and when he's engaged in a game. The exercise also makes him sleep better at night.*

Hanna: *Hanna says that, given her demanding schedule as single parent, nursing student, and direct-care staff member, she has little time for hobbies or other interests, but she does listen to music, go for walks, surf the Internet to find news of Ethiopia, and attend special religious services and celebrations. She likes going to the latter, because she can bring her children. Hanna talks about how she loved to play volleyball and field hockey as a young woman, and how she hopes to do so again one day.*

Ms. Oliver: *Ms. Oliver said she loved reading in the past but, because of her diminished eyesight, can no longer do this. However, she realized she could still enjoy books on tape, which her daughter would be happy to check out of the library for her.*

Sarah: *Sarah wishes to be more involved in community activities, such as joining a senior center or being on the board of the retirement community she lives in. She reckons the only thing that she'll get out of it is more interaction with people, something that she enjoys.*

Donna: *Donna learned that painting is actually a kind of meditation for her. It helps her focus in on the task at hand and avoid thinking about her problems.*

Rate your mood. Rate your mood here on a scale from 1 to 10: _____ .

EXERCISE: Explore Your Hobbies, Interests, and Activities

The following questions can help you identify the types of activities you currently enjoy, the ones you liked in the past, and ones that you're drawn to but haven't yet explored.

1. Think back to the last time you felt some pleasure or satisfaction in doing something that wasn't related to work. What were you doing?

_____

_____

_____

_____

2. Is this something that you do regularly or did regularly in the past?

_____

_____

_____

_____

3.   What kinds of qualities, skills, or behaviors do you have to show to be able to do these things? *Example:* Samantha said that knitting was an activity she used to enjoy. In reflecting on the resources this hobby required, she identified several. First, she had to *focus* to sit down and pay attention to what she was doing. Second, she had the *intelligence* and the *patience* to learn how to knit and to understand the patterns. Third, she had to have a certain level of *creativity*. She also had to have *support* to learn (a relative, friend, class, or a knitting group) or *resources* (the Internet or books). Finally, she had to have some *manual dexterity* to be able to manipulate the needles and yarn.

_____

_____

_____

_____

4.   What kinds of activities are you drawn to, although you have yet to try them?

_____

_____

_____

_____

Many depressed people have the following thoughts about hobbies or enjoyable activities:

•   *"I should be doing something more productive with my time."* Some depressed people find that they don't give themselves permission to relax and do the activities that give them pleasure. For example, Simone likes reading thrillers but doesn't let herself just lie back in the evenings and read, because she thinks she should be doing "worthwhile" activities, such as cleaning, paying bills, or organizing her paperwork.

•   *"Although I enjoy _____ [activity], there's no point in doing it, because I'm not any good at it."* If an activity gives you pleasure or satisfaction (and it doesn't hurt you or someone else), even if you can't earn money from it or gain recognition, the fact that it helps you feel better is its own reward.

•   *"Nothing sounds appealing."* This is the depression talking. Your thoughts are distorted when you're depressed, but in the actual moment of an experience, you'll likely find that it's better than you expected. You may also have to experiment to find hobbies or interests that make you feel at least slightly better.

After this discussion, if you give yourself permission to do something pleasurable but still find yourself unable to enjoy this new activity, you can explore some of your belief-system blocks (for example, "I don't deserve to relax and have fun") in chapter 8.

How Did This Exercise Help?

Having completed this exercise, rate your mood here on a scale from 1 to 10: _____ . How does this number differ from your initial rating? How do you account for any changes that you've made in your ratings?

_____

_____

_____

_____

Spirituality

I've alluded to spirituality in previous case examples, explaining that some people draw on belief in God or a higher power to cope with, or find a sense of meaning in, their depression. Some people have followed a particular religion since childhood; others feel alienated by their childhood religions and have sought alternative expression. Still others consider themselves "spiritual but not religious" and don't subscribe to any particular religious belief system, although they may find comfort in certain aspects of spiritual traditions. Additionally, you can view depression as a struggle with deep spiritual questions, such as wanting to find meaning in the world and a connection to a greater good. Viewing depression from this perspective, you may be able to find more meaning in the experience.

This section will help you identify and explore your own particular brand of spirituality and how it's helped you. Other people don't find that spirituality or religion helps them. For example, Ellen said that although she was married to a minister and had to play the role of minister's wife for many years, she doesn't find any particular solace from religion or a belief in God at this stage in her life.

On the other hand, Hanna says that if she starts to feel hopeless, she prays. She reports that prayer makes her feel that she's not alone and that God is beside her. If this doesn't lift her worry or sadness, she calls members of her prayer group for reassurance and support. She regularly attends a prayer group and services, and also attends church-sponsored events with her family.

Rate your mood. On a scale from 1 to 10, how do you feel now? _____ .

EXERCISE: Explore Your Spirituality

The following questions were sparked by Bertolino and O'Hanlon's (2002) ideas on spirituality.

1. What spiritual beliefs help you cope with difficulties?

_____

_____

_____

_____

2. Do you attend religious services regularly or otherwise engage in regular practices that fulfill you in a spiritual sense? How does this help you?

_____

_____

_____

_____

3. What spiritual practices (prayer, meditation, or other types of activities) do you follow? How do these help?

_____

_____

_____

_____

4. Now that you've identified your spiritual practices, how can you avail yourself more fully of your spiritual and religious resources to overcome your depression? *Example*: If you find that prayer lifts depression even just a little, you may decide to pray on a regular basis throughout the day. To remind herself to pray, Claire put up a sign, because in an onslaught of depressive feelings, she often became too consumed by them to remember any of her coping methods.

_____

_____

_____

_____

If you find that a certain practice gives you peace and calm, how can you increase the use of this practice in your daily life? For example, Kelly found that during a yoga class, her feelings of depression seemed less overwhelming. She decided to increase the number of weekly yoga classes she attended from two to four, so she could experience this more often. As another example, Delia mentioned that she went to a particular sanctuary in a park about once every three months, because it helped ease her tension; however, she realized that she could go more regularly since the experience had such a positive effect on her mood.

How Did This Exercise Help?

After completing this exercise, rate your mood here on a scale from 1 to 10: _____.
How does this number differ from your initial rating? What made the difference?

_____

_____

_____

_____

Survival of Abuse

I bring up abuse in this chapter on resilience for two reasons: First, a number of studies have indicated a significant relationship between depression and childhood physical and sexual abuse (Penza, Heim, and Nemeroff 2006), as well as intimate-partner violence as an adult

(Golding 1999). You may be one of these people who's been victimized in some way, and if so, it's likely playing a role in your depression. Second, if you've been a victim, you can examine how you were able to survive those difficult circumstances to find the strengths you've used or developed. Knowledge of the resilience you showed and your ways of handling these events can help you feel more empowered, and point you to the resources at your disposal to manage your problems now.

■ Case Examples

Hanna: *Hanna, a victim of intimate-partner violence, stated that sometimes she would run out of the house and sleep in the car with the doors locked when her husband became violent. After he bought a remote door opener so he could unlock the door to hurt her, she escaped to the neighbors to call the police.*

Hanna said that the experience showed how she was resourceful: if one thing didn't work, she tried another avenue. She could apply the same level of resourcefulness to tackling her depression by trying the different exercises presented in this workbook.

Hanna said her husband's abuse began not long after they married. She put up with it for many years, because she'd been taught in her culture that a good wife tolerates abuse and infidelity. Several factors acted together, though, to get her to leave the abusive situation. First, the abuse didn't stop, as she'd hoped. Then, after coming to America, she learned that abuse wasn't tolerated. She also learned that intimate-partner violence hurts the children as well; even if they're not being hit, their witnessing violence can be detrimental to them.

Upon reflecting on her qualities and supports that got her to leave the situation, Hanna said that just the process of getting in touch with these qualities helped her see herself as more capable and empowered, and that she could get past the depression as she had other problems in her life. She noted that she possessed intelligence to be able to learn about how domestic violence was viewed in this culture. She could use her intelligence now to grasp principles presented in this workbook and to do the exercises. Second, she overcame a major cultural stigma about leaving a marital partner, even one who was abusive or unhealthy. That took a tremendous amount of courage and meant she had to stand up to people in her family and community who said it was worth staying with a man who was abusive if he was a good provider. When applying this experience to her depression, she considered her traditional cultural view of depression; it meant that you were "crazy," and it was shameful not only to yourself but also to your family. Because of her ability to change her cultural views on violence toward women, Hanna was open-minded about considering another view of depression. She learned that in the United States, it's considered a clinical condition that affects many people and can be successfully treated. This view helped her see that she could seek assistance from a therapist or her doctor in order to feel better.

Hanna also showed courage to stand up to her husband and express that she would no longer play victim to his violence. Her courage could be used to tackle any issues she needed to address for her depression or to seek further help. Hanna said she took advantage of the resources that were available in America—laws protecting people from abuse and the use of a shelter for battered women—noting that even though the resources were there, she had to be empowered to avail herself of them. The same personal empowerment is necessary to be able to take advantage of treatments available for depression, such as books and workbooks (like this one), psychotherapists, and psychiatrists.

Adele: *Adele's a young woman stuck in a relationship with a man who abuses drugs and alcohol, and emotionally manipulates her. She said that when she's with her boyfriend, she tends to buy into what he tells her, but when she talks to her friends, they give her a more realistic picture of his manipulations. She noted that it helps to maintain contact with "reality" by having her friends to rely on for support, even though that hasn't enabled her to leave the relationship yet. She says, "I think it's a matter of time before I'll be able to leave him, but I won't be able to do it without my friends' support." She also credits her "smarts" with resisting her boyfriend's constant pressure to move in with him. She recognizes that she'll be even more "ensnared" if she doesn't maintain her own apartment.*

Adele realizes that her intelligence, her courage in standing up to her boyfriend (when he pressures her about moving in together), and her social support have helped her deal with a situation that likely contributes to her depression. Getting in touch with these resources and supports helps her view herself as more capable and empowered than she previously believed. She can draw on these resources of courage, intelligence, and social support when she's ready to leave the relationship and face the depression she fears will arise once she's alone.

James: *James said that while growing up in an abusive family, he relied on his friends to get him out of a bad situation at home. Even in junior high school, he spent a lot of time at his friends' houses. As a result, he gained good social skills and the ability to form friendships easily. Even as an adult, he found it important to spend time with his friends, because for him, they're family. James's social network and his ability to connect with people could be important elements in his recovery from depression.*

From growing up in his family, James primarily learned to "rely on myself," because he couldn't count on his family to take care of him. He admitted that there were both good and bad aspects to "relying on myself." James is very competent, works hard, and has a lot of what's known in psychological terms as self-efficacy: "If I set my mind to do something, I know I can do it," he says. "But at times, it hasn't been good. I'm my best when I'm the boss or working alone. I don't do that well taking orders from other people who are 'idiots.' In relationships, I'm too independent, I'm told, and don't ask for help easily."

Rate your mood. Rate on a scale from 1 to 10 how you feel now: _____ .

EXERCISE: Explore Any Past Abuse
You've Experienced

1. Think of a time when you were in an abusive situation and were threatened but managed to escape or avoid harm, even just temporarily. How did you do that?

_____

_____

_____

_____

2. What does your answer to the previous question show about you? How can you apply these same resources to your problems now?

_____

_____

_____

_____

3. If you were able to leave an abusive situation in the past, how were you able to do this?

_____

_____

_____

4. Consider an abusive or extremely challenging situation that you went through or are currently experiencing that was or is out of your control. Think about how you were or are able to survive. It's likely that you've drawn on both positive and negative ways of coping. For now, jot down any unhealthy coping methods in the space provided; you'll address them in chapter 6.

_____

_____

_____

_____

5.   What did you do in this situation?

_____

_____

_____

_____

6.   What did you say to yourself?

_____

_____

_____

_____

7.   How were you able to seek help from others or gain support?

_____

_____

_____

_____

8.   What qualities in yourself did you draw on?

_____

_____

_____

_____

9. What spiritual resources did you draw upon to survive the situation?

_____

_____

_____

_____

10. How did you decide to behave differently than those who hurt you? How have you been able to do this?

_____

_____

_____

_____

11. Did you resort to any unhealthy coping methods? If so, list them here.

_____

_____

_____

_____

How Did This Exercise Help?

After completing this exercise, rate your mood here on a scale from 1 to 10: _____.
How does this number differ from your initial rating? What changed?

_____

_____

_____

_____

Employment

Exploring your current place of employment or your employment history is important, because it can pinpoint strengths, supports, and resources that you may have overlooked. A résumé is particularly good for a depressed person to contemplate, because it highlights the aspects of yourself that aren't depressed. A résumé highlights your strengths and accomplishments. Similarly, people don't go to job interviews to discuss their depression. They instead put forward the enthusiastic and responsible parts of themselves, and they display a sense of their own worth, by trying to "sell" themselves to a prospective employer. Instead of downplaying those aspects, you can become aware that these are parts of yourself that can be expanded. This process shows that you aren't defined by your depression.

▪ *Case Examples*

Josephine: *Josephine, a twenty-eight-year-old African American woman, explained that while she was living in a shelter after leaving her husband, she heard that a tow-truck company was hiring. Initially, she doubted she'd get the job, because she didn't have experience. However, at the interview she described herself as "determined and someone who always arrives on time and does the job right without taking shortcuts."*

The most difficult part of her job was the training. At first, she found it difficult to operate the tow truck, but after a few days she got the hang of it. Josephine reported that she loved her job because of the driving. She said that driving relaxed her; she could turn up the music and enjoy herself.

In reflecting on the strengths she showed in this employment setting, Josephine identified several:

- *The willingness to take risks (she didn't have the experience but decided to apply anyway)*

- *Her determination and sense of responsibility, which sold her employer on hiring her*

- *Her persistence in learning a new skill*

- *The ability to derive satisfaction from her job*

Mrs. Ayela: *Despite having had only a ninth-grade education in her native land and having been forced to write with her nondominant hand in school, Mrs. Ayela is now the office manager of a large cleaning service. "In my last job, I received computer training and personnel management training. After they reduced personnel and I was laid off, I applied to this job. I felt confident with the computer, and I dressed professionally for the interview. I was also flexible about being available to work nights."*

When asked what she found to be most challenging or difficult about her job, Mrs. Ayela responded, "To deal with my bosses is difficult, because I need to control what I say. I say what I think, which creates problems sometimes, but it also means I take charge when I need to. If I say something out of line, I try to excuse myself and leave the scene. I can apologize too."

When asked what kept her at her job, Mrs. Ayela wrote, "I like to be in charge. A lot of people depend on me to keep the schedule straight, to organize their time efficiently, and to get paid." In addressing the skills and qualities her employer sees in her, Mrs. Ayela recounted, "I stay overtime until the job is done. If there's something to be done, I don't wait for someone else to do it—I do it. For instance, if an office building needs cleaning, and not enough people show up, I go ahead and clean too. I supervise forty workers. Every day, I solve problems, deal with any customer complaints, and see that everyone does his or her job." In reflecting on her strengths, Mrs. Ayela identified her professionalism, flexibility, willingness to take charge and pitch in, and management skills.

Peter: *Peter said that he played video games to escape from his depression and, after leaving the military, considered owning his own video game store. He was looking for something that could give him passion for life, and video gaming was one of the few activities that excited him. He decided he could look into this option by learning how to run a business from doing research on the Internet and at the library, and possibly also investigating continuing-education courses offered on the topic.*

Rate your mood. Rate your mood here on a scale from 1 to 10: _____ .

EXERCISE: Explore Your Employment History

1. How did you sell yourself in your résumé and job interview to get the job?

_____

_____

_____

_____

2. What did you tell your current or most recent employer that might have contributed to your being hired?

_____

_____

3. Think of a recent situation, or one that stands out in your mind, at work when you were proud of the way you handled something. What did you do?

_____

_____

_____

4. What did you say to yourself?

_____

_____

_____

5. What do you think your boss, coworkers, or customers thought about you in that situation?

_____

_____

_____

6. What does how you handled this situation say about you?

_____

_____

_____

7. Think of a recent difficult situation in your job or one that stands out in your mind. How did you meet or work toward meeting that challenge?

_____

_____

_____

_____

8. What goals do you have related to your career or job?

_____

_____

_____

_____

9. List the strengths you've identified in this section that you can apply to your current problems. For instance, if you can schedule your time well at work, you can schedule your own unstructured time when feeling your worst. If you can listen well to others at work, perhaps you can listen to yourself and validate your own struggles with the same level of empathy. If you can effectively solve problems at work, how can you approach your own problems in a similar way?

_____

_____

_____

_____

How Did This Exercise Help?

After completing this exercise, rate your mood here on a scale from 1 to 10: _____ . How does this number differ from your initial rating? What did you learn?

_____

_____

Parenting

If you're a parent, you know you have to dig down deep to find the personal resources that you need to take care of children. You also might consciously develop such qualities, for example, patience, creativity, and knowledge of child development.

■ *Case Examples*

Delia: *When considering what her children would say makes her a good parent, Delia wrote that it depended on the particular child. Her son loved it when she did something physical with him, such as sledding or helping him learn how to ride his bike. Her daughter liked coloring and making cards with her mother.*

Claire: *Claire found it difficult to deal with her two-year-old's defiant behaviors, such as hitting his brother and her, spitting, and failing to follow her directions. She handled this challenge by venting her frustrations to those close to her. She joked about her son's misbehavior. She discussed with her husband what to do about the situation and watched parenting shows on television, like* Supernanny. *She also tried a number of different strategies. For instance, she offered rewards for good behavior (such as stars and the promise of a bike) and punishment for bad behavior (such as not being allowed to go places or having to do a time-out). When he didn't stay in time-out and laughed at her efforts to put him there, she used his crib to keep him in one place. When he learned to climb out of the crib, she restrained him in place.*

Claire had initially decided that she wouldn't have children, because she didn't want to hurt anyone since she'd been hurt by her father's depression. However, when Claire eventually entered into a good relationship and got married, she changed her decision, because her new husband so wanted to have children. After the decision was made, along with it came the commitment to do a better job than her parents had done. Claire said that she's been able to do this, because she has a good relationship with her husband, who's a supportive partner (whereas her parents' marriage was abusive and conflictual); she has financial resources that she's willing to spend on part-time child care so that she's not overwhelmed from the demands of taking care of young children; and she avails herself of playgroups and classes for her children to structure their time. She also has a career that she's been able to keep up with despite having children, whereas her own mother was a full-time homemaker who lacked stimulation, and was lonely and frustrated as a result.

Evelyn: *Evelyn said that her mother used to call her "bad," "mean," and "hateful" as a child, which was very hurtful to her. Evelyn decided that when she corrected her children, she would focus on the behavior ("you weren't listening") rather than refer to their personhood ("you're bad").*

Rate your mood. Rate your mood here on a scale from 1 to 10: _____ .

EXERCISE: Explore Your Parenting Skills

These questions ask about the strengths and resources it takes to parent children.

1. What do you think your children would say makes you a good parent? You'll have to think hypothetically here, because unless your children are grown up, they probably can't answer in a helpful way.

   _____

   _____

   _____

   _____

2. When do you think you're able to be your best as a parent? Think about a recent situation, or one that stands out in your mind, in which you were proud of your parenting. What did you do? What did you say to your children? How did your children react to you?

   _____

   _____

   _____

   _____

3. Think about a recent situation, or one that stands out in your mind, when you really enjoyed your children. What did you do? What did you say to them? How did your children react to you?

   _____

   _____

4. Recall a recent parenting challenge. What qualities, behaviors, beliefs, and supports have you drawn on? What qualities, behaviors, beliefs, and supports have developed as a result?

_____

_____

_____

5. As a parent, how have you decided to behave differently from your own parents? How have you made that happen? Think about a recent situation that you handled differently than your parents did. What did you do and say? What did you say to yourself?

_____

_____

_____

6. Next, you'll use the responses you wrote in this section. List all the resources and strengths—your qualities, behaviors, things you say to yourself, and supports—that have either developed as a result of parenting or that you draw on to effectively parent. For instance, most parents are compelled to become more patient and nurturing. If you're a parent, you've probably learned to put someone else's needs before your own. Perhaps you've also developed empathy for other parents, because the "job" is so stressful. You've likely acquired a lot of knowledge on child care and child development. You may have developed a sense of hope for the future by helping your children look forward to events. You likely experience at least moments of joy when your children are particularly delightful. As in Claire's example, many people meet other parents and expand their social network in this way.

_____

_____

How Did This Exercise Help?

After completing this exercise, rate your mood here on a scale from 1 to 10: _____ . How does this number differ from your initial rating? How do you account for any changes that were made in your ratings?

_____

_____

_____

_____

PUTTING IT ALL TOGETHER

This chapter has focused on resilience, which is about the strengths you show despite life's difficulties—and the strengths you've developed precisely because of facing these challenges. *Resilience theory* recognizes that people face risk factors (hardships) but also have protective factors (strengths) to help mitigate any risk. For the purpose of your depression, you can work on reducing your risk factors, or at least how to cope with the stressors you face. You can also work to enhance your strengths. First, you have to learn what your strengths are, and in this chapter, you've thoroughly examined the strengths you show in various aspects of your life (such as your hobbies, employment, and relationships) and in resolving past problems and difficulties. Now, in the next exercise, you have the opportunity to capture these strengths by listing them together and seeing how they can be applied to beat your depression and other life stressors. Go through each of the previous exercises and pull out what you wrote down that's relevant to what you're facing today, organizing your strengths into the following categories:

- Thinking resources

- Personal qualities

- Activities

- Informal support (friends and family; community)

- Formal support

This list can be cut out or copied and kept in a convenient place to remind you of your skills. The first chart is an example that shows how Samantha filled out her chart.

SAMANTHA'S SUMMARY CHART OF STRENGTHS

Identified Strength	How to Apply to Problem Situation
Thinking Resources • *I always find a way to make it through.* • *Everything works out for the best in the end.* • *I have a lot going for me.*	• *Repeat these statement when I'm feeling bad.*
Personal Qualities • *Intelligence* • *Good listening skills* • *Caring about my dogs*	• *Can use my mind to help me do the exercises in the workbook.* • *Friends whom I've listened to are available to listen to me too.* • *Means that I probably matter to some human creatures.*
Activities • *Knitting* • *Walking the dogs* • *Watching DVDs*	• *Knitting is something I can do when I feel bad. It distracts me from the way I feel, plus I have something to show for my bad mood.* • *Gives me exercise and I know the dogs enjoy it.* • *I can relax and lose myself if the movie's good.*
Informal Support (Friends and Family) *I have two friends that I can call when I'm feeling very bad.*	*Although I can call them to talk to them about how I feel when I'm unhappy, I can also go out somewhere with one of them and take the initiative to ward off a bad mood.*

Informal Support (Community)	• Visiting church when no one's there so I can feel some peace and pray.
• I don't like going to formal church services. It doesn't do anything for me, but I do like the quiet and peacefulness associated with churches.	• I can take a "cooking for one" class at the local community recreation center, so I can eat better and take better care of myself.
Formal Support	• I could visit a psychiatrist or a psychotherapist again. I've been told that I might have to try different people to find one that I connect with.
• I visited a therapist on a couple of occasions in the past. One was helpful and one wasn't.	

The following blank chart is for you to fill out.

SUMMARY CHART OF STRENGTHS

Identified Strength	How to Apply to Problem Situation
Thinking Resources	
Personal Qualities	
Activities	
Informal Support (Friends and Family)	
Informal Support (Community)	
Formal Support	

CONCLUSION

Listing your accumulated strengths highlights the positive attributes you bring, the actions you take, and the supports you've formed. You'll note from the emphasis on the efforts you've made in various life domains that you aren't defined by your depression. Eliciting and emphasizing the existence of these resources through the previous exercises likely might help you feel more competent and worthy. Feeling better about yourself, in turn, helps chip away at the low self-esteem characteristic of depression. By highlighting your assets, you can use them strategically to circumvent your depression.

CHAPTER 3

Looking Toward a Brighter Future

One of the most difficult aspects of depression is the loss of hope that accompanies it. When you're enveloped in depression, it's hard to see beyond it. Depression colors your perspective in negative ways: it seems as if you've always been depressed and you'll always be depressed, that there'll be no end to the pain, and that nothing will get better. You may find it hard to believe, but this isn't necessarily the reality of the situation. For example, Barbara talked about how she'd been depressed for years, when, actually, months had gone by when she wasn't depressed and was satisfied with her life. The problem with hopelessness, along with how painful it is to feel this way, is that it may prevent you from doing the things you can to help yourself feel better, such as the exercises in this workbook. It may also give you justification for doing things that are decidedly *unhelpful*. For instance, people who've "given up" may say to themselves, "So what if I drink (or use drugs or overeat)? Nothing's going to help me anyway, so I might as well feel better any way I can."

By going through the previous two chapters and exploring your resources for managing your depression symptoms and the strengths you bring to various life domains, you may have emerged with a changed view of yourself and the past. You may now see your life in more balanced terms by focusing not only on your problems and your depression but also on all the resources you've used in all the different domains of your life and throughout your life to overcome difficulties. All of this work may have given you some hope for the future, as well.

This chapter will continue the work of helping you find hope for your future. As part of this aim, you'll spend time constructing a view of a nondepressed future. Although this may sound like an alien concept at this point, I'll take you step by step through the process of how to do this.

Rate your level of hopefulness. Before getting into this material, take the time to rate your mood now on a variation of the mood-rating scale previously used. Rate your sense of hope on a scale from 1 to 10, in which 10 means "very hopeful." Put your rating here: _____ .

WHAT GIVES YOU HOPE?

Many people say that their children give them hope, because they're the next generation and new life, and they provide an opportunity to do things differently. For some people, belief in a higher power and spirituality gives them hope, even if it's for an afterlife promising that things won't be so difficult.

Sometimes people say they have no hope of feeling any better, but there are often aspects to their narratives that we can tease out to find the "hidden hope." For example, Sandra, a forty-year-old woman, said that she'd been on at least ten different antidepressants since she'd been depressed, for about twenty years. She professed to feel no hope that she would feel any better. However, we can view her tendency to keep trying different medications, even though she says none of them have helped, as a sign that she believes that one day she'll feel better. When Sandra was asked, "Why do you keep trying? Why don't you resign yourself to the fact that you'll always feel how you do now?" she realized that she did believe that something could help her. She hadn't given up hope that she could feel better.

Some people experience a sense of hope from what other people tell them. Donna, a forty-one-year-old whose ex-husband had cheated on her, used her money for drugs and alcohol, and ruined her credit, said she was finding it difficult settling into her new apartment. She couldn't afford furniture, and was unused to the silence and solitude. Life with her ex-husband had been chaotic, but now she was finding being alone very difficult and depressing. She confided in a coworker about her feelings, and he responded that he'd gone through a divorce after fifteen years of marriage and three children. He said that having a hard time dealing with the silence had been a difficult challenge for him too. He'd coped with it by turning up the volume on the television or stereo. When the apartment he lived in became too oppressive, he took out the trash just to change the scene a little. He'd coped with sleeping alone by stacking up pillows behind his back so that he felt a "presence" behind him. Donna felt enormously comforted by what her coworker had told her, because it showed that she wasn't losing her mind. She understood that feeling lonely and having difficulty tolerating the silence was a natural adjustment after losing a relationship. She said she'd also felt reassured by her coworker's indication that this period of time only lasted for a few months, and she realized that she just had to go through it but that it would end soon.

Attending 12-step groups can give you an enormous sense of hope, because you'll hear stories of redemption; people who "hit rock bottom" through drinking and drug use will talk about how they turned their lives around. Some people find hope in hearing these stories; even if they're not alcoholics or drug addicts, they can see that life can change in surprising ways, even if it seems completely hopeless.

Many people experience hope for the future through their children. They know they have to keep going and do the best they can so that their children will do well.

EXERCISE: Find Your Sense of Hopefulness

1. Now that you've read some examples, write here what gives you hope that you'll feel better. *Hint:* The fact that you're reading this workbook says that you're trying to do what you can and have hope that your efforts will help.

_____

_____

_____

_____

2. Think about a recent time when you felt a little more hopeful than usual. What happened?

_____

_____

_____

_____

3. What did you do?

_____

_____

_____

_____

4.   What did you tell yourself?

_____

_____

_____

_____

5.   What supports did you draw on?

_____

_____

_____

_____

6.   In what ways can you replicate some of the things in that situation: what you did, what you told yourself, the supports you drew on?

_____

_____

_____

_____

Rerate your sense of hopefulness. On a scale from 1 to 10, in which 10 means "very hopeful," how hopeful do you feel after doing this exercise? Write your answer here: _____. What changed?

_____

_____

_____

_____

A NONDEPRESSED FUTURE

The aim of this section is to help you envision your future without depression. (Future-oriented questions were originally devised by solution-focused writers [de Shazer 1988]). Why is it important to consider a depression-free future? First, it orients you to where you want to be, rather than allowing you to remain stuck in rumination about how bad you feel now. As discussed in chapter 2, rumination is one of the most unproductive ways of coping with depression. Second, the future-oriented questions that you'll be asked in this chapter will help you to see some alternatives to depression. Third, when you see where you want to be, you can start to develop a map for how to get there.

Rate your sense of hopefulness: Before getting into this material, take the time to assess your mood now on a variation of the mood-rating scale. Assess your sense of hopefulness on a scale from 1 to 10, in which 10 means "very hopeful." Write your rating here: _____.

EXERCISE: Envision Your Life Without Depression

What will your life look like once you've gone through this workbook and successfully emerged from depression? In other words, let's say you no longer feel depressed, and it's a thing of the past. Please read the following case example and guidelines before completing this exercise.

1. What will you be doing?

   _____

   _____

   _____

   _____

2. Who would be the first person to notice a difference in you? What would he or she notice about you that's different?

   _____

   _____

   _____

71

3. What will you say to the people around you? How will you say it?

_____

_____

_____

_____

4. How will they respond to you?

_____

_____

_____

_____

5. What will you say to yourself?

_____

_____

_____

_____

■ *Case Example: Talia*

Talia, a thirty-four-year-old single mother, answered these questions in the following way: "I'll wake up after a good night's sleep. I'll think, 'Oh look, the sun is shining. It looks like it'll be a nice day.' I'll smile and hug my children when I see them. I'll have energy to face the day, and I'll make breakfast for me and the kids. They'll be the first ones to notice the change in me. They'll notice that I'm smiling and moving around. I'll be proud when they play and shout, because I'll know that they're happy, healthy kids. But I'll also be able to be consistent when they refuse to get ready. I'll be able to follow through with taking away privileges or enforcing a time-out, instead of giving in to them and then screaming my head off. We'll get to school on time, and then I'll come home and clean up. I'll get all my errands done and feel pleased that my life is ordered and that I can get the things done that I need to. I'll call my mother on the phone and end the call politely if she starts to tell me what to do. I'll have a shower, and then enjoy coffee and the newspaper. When the kids come home, I'll feel replenished from my time alone and play with them, enjoying how happy they are to have my attention. I'll have set up a playdate for them ahead of time, so I can have some socializing time with other moms in the afternoon."

Guidelines

1. The word "will," as in "what will your life look like," might've snagged your attention. After all, how can you know what your life will look like? However, this language is used purposively, because language shapes the way we think (Berg 1994). "Will" is a definitive term; rather than hedging, it implies that change will happen. Using definitive wording such as "will" sets up certainty in your mind that change can occur.

2. Get as specific as you can about this vision of a nondepressed future. Note that in the example of Talia, she doesn't just say, "I will feel better." The picture shows not only how Talia "feels" but also her new behaviors and thoughts.

   The additional prompts to the exercise are designed to help you get to the concrete behaviors rather than stay at the level of generalities. Also, when you construct this vision, imagine that you're being taped by a video recorder. What would the camera "see" you doing?

3. Although ultimately you want to feel better, I ask you to focus on thoughts and behaviors. Why? It's easier to change your thoughts and behaviors than your feelings. By changing your thoughts and the actions you take, you influence how you feel.

4. Phrase your description in terms of the presence of positives rather than the absence of negatives. Write about what you want in your life rather than what you don't want. Notice that in the example, Talia focuses on what she wants to see (such as waking up and seeing that the weather's nice and thinking that it might be a nice day) rather than the absence of negatives (such as, "I won't just lie there exhausted, wondering how I'm going to get through the day on such little sleep, thinking about all the stuff I have to do and how I don't want to do any of it"). It's important to orient to where you want to go rather than to endlessly ruminate on your depressed feelings.

5. Keep your vision fairly realistic. For instance, sometimes people jump to the answer, "I'll have won the lottery." Even if you insist on going there, you can still get down to the specifics of the situation with questions like these: "What would I do?" "What would I say to those around me?"

6. If you have a hard time with these questions, recall the following prompts:

    •   Tell yourself, "I know that I don't know, so I can just make it up."

    •   Ask yourself, "What would _____ [an important person in your life who knows you well] say I would do?"

How Did This Exercise Help?

After completing the exercise, how would you rate your sense of hopefulness now on a scale from 1 to 10? _____ How does this number differ from your initial rating? What do you think contributed to any change?

_____

_____

_____

_____

EXERCISE: What to Do the Next Time You Feel Depressed

When you feel bad, it's hard not to wallow in how terrible you feel, although it's sometimes detrimental to your mood. To build on the prior exercise of envisioning a nondepressed future, this exercise asks you to project yourself into a nondepressed state even if you currently feel acutely depressed.

1. Rate your mood on a scale from 1 to 10, in which 10 means "fine" and 1 means "totally miserable": _____ .

2. Write down not what you're currently experiencing but what you'd like to experience instead.

    a. What would you like to do instead?

    _____

    _____

b. What would you like to say to yourself instead?

_____

_____

_____

c. What would you like to say to other people? How would you say it?

_____

_____

_____

d. What would other people notice about you?

_____

_____

_____

Rerate your mood. Rerate your mood on the mood scale: _____. How does this number differ from your initial rating? What do you think has contributed to any changes?

_____

_____

_____

_____

SCALING QUESTIONS

Scaling questions originated from solution-focused therapy and continue in the vein of exploring a nondepressed future (de Jong and Berg 2008). But they also involve how you can get there. The following steps are included in scaling questions:

1. Choose your goal.

2.   Define "10," or what success means.

3.   Define where you are now.

4.   Change your viewpoint.

5.   Set up tasks for yourself.

6.   Measure your progress.

Choose Your Goal

The scale you'll construct will center on your goal of feeling better (such as "feeling happier"). Or, you can work on a goal for a problem that you believe underlies your depression (such as "getting along better with people" or "making more friends"). Here are some questions to orient you toward a goal you might pick:

1.   What's a current major stressor for you?

_____

_____

_____

_____

2.   What two or three things would have to change to lessen your stress or make this situation better?

_____

_____

_____

_____

3.   What will tell you that things are better?

_____

_____

---

4.   What will show you that working through the exercises in this book has been successful?

In keeping oriented to what you're working toward rather than what you're trying to change, it's important to phrase any goal you choose in a positive way. For example, rather than "My goal is to not be so lonely," a positive goal might be "I want to make two new friends." Your goal should be realistically attainable, rather than rely on everything in your life being perfect. Life being what it is, it'll never be perfect; however, you can learn to work within its parameters and still feel okay. Write your goal in detail, and make sure it's a goal that you can easily measure; that is, it should be easy to tell when you reach your goal. Here are some other sample goals:

- Get a new job.

- Exercise regularly.

- Find a hobby.

Name your goal here: _____ .

Define "10"

Now we'll use the following scale to develop a way to measure your progress toward your goal. Next, you'll name three types of behaviors you could see yourself engaging in when you've reached "10." Again, it's important to focus on what you want rather than what you don't want.

1.   What thoughts will you have when you've reached your goal? *Examples:* "Life's all right." "I can handle what comes my way." "Things are looking up."

Thought #1:

_____

_____

Thought #2:

_____

_____

_____

Thought #3:

_____

_____

_____

2.   What will you do when you've reached your goal? *Examples:* Playing tennis once a week in a league, taking a cooking class, applying for jobs, doing volunteer work, or seeing more of your family and friends. Note that these are actions you're taking, not events that are happening to you from the outside. For instance, if you're tempted to answer, "Have a boyfriend" or "Be married," these are events that are, to some extent, outside of your control. To turn the response into a more manageable answer, ask instead, "What will I do when I have a boyfriend?" Selma realized that one of the reasons why she wanted a boyfriend was to have a person to go with to explore the surrounding area on weekend day trips. Even without a boyfriend, she could make this happen by inviting other single girlfriends on weekend outings or joining a social group (such as a hiking group that explored different trails).

_____

_____

_____

_____

Define Where You Are Now

Now that you've defined "10" on your scale, rate your current progress toward your goal on this scale from 1 ("very low or seldom") to 10 ("I do or say these things all the time" or "I feel that I'm already living this goal"). Rating: _____

People often place themselves at a number above 1, implying that there's already progress in their lives toward their goals. When you've done this, ask yourself, "What have I done to be at _____ [your rating]? What resources have I used to get to this place?"

_____

_____

_____

_____

Barbara rates her progress toward her goal at 2. She said she felt that her neighbors, with whom she talked daily and socialized on the weekends, kept her going. She also spent three days a week with her physically handicapped grown daughter. This supplied her with needed companionship. Finally, the fact that she had three grandchildren whom she loved dearly brightened her life. Her visits to them also kept her spirits up.

Occasionally, people place their progress at 1. If you've done this, ask yourself, "What am I doing to prevent my problems from getting even worse?"

_____

_____

_____

_____

The fact that your situation isn't as bad as it could be means that you're taking steps to ensure that it doesn't get worse. Steven rated his progress at 1, because in order to deal with his depression, he'd been using cocaine and alcohol on a daily basis for the past year. He was having sinus problems because of the cocaine use and was spending all his savings on drugs and alcohol. He said he didn't know how he was going to stop. When asked, "What are you doing to prevent your problems from getting even worse?" he said he prayed to God to help him; he still went to his job every day, no matter how bad he felt; and at least he didn't have a wife and children to "bring down."

Change Your Viewpoint

You can change your viewpoint by putting yourself in the perspective of another person and rating your progress toward your goal on the same scale from that person's viewpoint. Very often people view themselves differently from how others experience them, and in general, people with depression see themselves as less worthy and competent than how others view them. Being pushed to examine your progress from another person's perspective may help you to see it more realistically.

For example, Barbara admitted that her daughter Petra would probably rate her progress higher, perhaps at 4. Petra would say that Barbara was well off financially and didn't have to work; she could afford anything she wanted. Barbara socialized a lot, went to the beauty parlor every week, and went out to eat at restaurants a few times each week, plus she attended concerts and movies each weekend.

1. Name a person who knows you well: _____.
    Where would that person place your progress on the scale? _____ How would that person account for this number? What does this person see you doing? What does this person know about you that would tell him or her this?

    _____

    _____

    _____

    _____

2. If there's a discrepancy between your rating and the hypothetical rating of another person, explore what you see as the difference between your perspective and that of this person who knows you well.

    _____

    _____

    _____

    _____

Barbara realized from doing this exercise that she did have more in her life than she'd first considered. She found that she lived a life of ease and participated in many enjoyable activities throughout the week.

Set Up Tasks for Yourself

People who are depressed are often overwhelmed by their problems and what needs to get done. Daunted by the enormity of the tasks that face them, depressed people sometimes give up ("It's too much; I can't do it") and withdraw or avoid their problems, becoming virtually paralyzed. As you may already know, this response may end up making you feel even worse. For example, Greta realized that she would probably feel better if she got a new job. Even though she knew that that's what she should do, she couldn't face doing it. One major reason is that so many different tasks make up such a complex goal as "finding a new job."

The antidote when you're feeling overwhelmed is to break down problems and tasks into baby steps. In the example of finding a job, this might be Greta's list:

1. Search Internet site #1 for jobs.

2. Search Internet site #2 for jobs.

3. Call my friend at the agency to see if they're hiring there.

4. Go to company #1's website to see if they have employment postings.

5. Go to company #2's website to see if they have employment postings.

6. Go to company #3's website to see if they have employment postings.

7. Search the classifieds in Sunday's paper.

8. Update my résumé.

9. E-mail my friend to ask her if I can use her as a reference.

10. Call for more information on that company I thought of today.

11. Get the address of the company I worked for two years ago.

12. Fill out application #1.

13. Send application #1.

14. Fill out application #2.

15. Send application #2.

16. Fill out application #3.

17. Send application #3.

Break your goal down into baby steps.

1.

2.

3.

4.

5.

6.

7.

8.

9.

10.

As well as being able to take steps toward solving manageable problems, it's also important to be able to generate solutions to problems. Perhaps you don't yet know how to go about meeting your goal. Many times, people who are depressed are unable to come up with options. Depression shuts down their ability to think effectively. They may instead go round and round in their minds without coming to resolution. This contributes to their sense of being stuck and belief that there's no hope.

The term for coming up with a list of possible solutions when you're faced with a stressor or a problem is called *brainstorming* (D'Zurilla and Nezu 2001), a skill that you'll learn here.

To get the process started, ask "how" or "what" (not "why") questions: "How can I get more meaning in my life?" "How can I have fun in my life without alcohol?" "How can I meet more people?" Come up with as many solutions as possible, even those that are silly, outlandish, or impossible. Here are some prompts to get ideas going if you get stuck:

- What would _____ [an important person your life] say you might do about this?

- What would _____ [someone you look up to, or a hero] say you might do about this?

- Think about what you've done to solve other problems like this in the past.

At this juncture, refrain from criticizing the options you come up with. Just focus on creating as many possibilities as you can.

Take one of the problems you named, particularly one in which you feel stuck. Note it here: _____ . Now come up with as many ways to solve this problem as possible:

1.

2.

3.

4.

5.

6.

7.

8.

9.

10.

For the purpose of the scaling questions, think about which of the solutions you could implement in either of your two lists that would move you one number on the scale closer to your goal. What's one step you can take? Barbara identified that she could call the Jewish Community Services Center and find out about social activities for seniors.

Now that you've identified the goal you want to work on, you can continue to work toward it, identifying one step at a time. If you feel unmotivated to take even one small step toward your goal, you might want to go back and change your scale, basing it on "feeling motivated" about tackling your goal, and then follow the same steps. For further work on building motivation, also see part II.

Measure Your Progress

You can rate your progress from time to time (say weekly) as you continue to work on your scale, dating each rating as you go. For now, rate your progress on a scale from 1 to 10: _____ . How does this number differ from your previous rating? What do you think has contributed to any changes?

_____

_____

_____

_____

CONCLUSION

This chapter has oriented you toward change and helped you envision a time when depression is no longer a problem for you. This work can help you develop a blueprint for how you'll make such a future a reality. With the scaling questions, you may have also gotten in touch with the strengths and resources you've called upon to help yourself feel better and make progress toward your goals. A premise of solution-focused therapy, a strengths-based model that undergirds the approach taken in this workbook, is that small change can snowball into more positive change. By taking specific steps to change your circumstances and mood, small shifts in the way you see yourself (as more competent, as more empowered) will occur and people will respond to you differently. These positive changes lead to further changes in the way you feel about yourself and the actions you take.

CHAPTER 4

Exceptions to Depression

This final chapter in the strengths-based section of this book will help you explore what are known in solution-focused therapy as *exceptions*, times when the problem (the depression) isn't there (deJong and Berg 2008). When you can identify these situations and explore what went into making them happen, you can figure out how to help yourself feel better.

CAPTURING MOMENTS OF HAPPINESS

Many depressed people can't conceive of feeling "happy." The purpose of this section is to show you that you do experience at least momentary happiness on occasion. Most people, even those who aren't depressed, don't feel elation—a state of intense happiness—on a regular basis. However, they do experience the many shades of happiness that are also available to you:

- Pleasure (watching a kitten play)

- Enjoyment (reveling in a hot bath or shower)

- Satisfaction (finishing a task)

- A sense of mastery (completing a difficult project)

- Relief (finishing a task you'd dreaded)

- Gratitude (when someone, even a stranger, unexpectedly does something nice for you in some small way, such as opening the door for you, picking up something you've dropped, or catching up to you to return something you inadvertently left behind in a cafe or on the subway)

The purpose of noticing these approximations of happiness is this: first, to show you that, contrary to your biased thinking process, you do experience these feelings; second, by focusing on these experiences, you can enlarge upon their importance; and third, you can study these occurrences to find your own prescription for happiness.

EXERCISE: Notice Your Moments of Happiness

For the next week, list five experiences of happiness you have each day. Don't overlook even very small, fleeting, or minor feelings. Each day, assess the impact of doing this exercise on the way you feel.

Monday

Rate your mood. Before starting the exercise today, rate your mood on a scale from 1 to 10, in which 1 means "miserable" and 10 means "good." Put your rating here: _____ .

I felt _____ ,

because _____ .

I felt _____ ,

because _____ .

I felt _____ ,

because _____ .

I felt _____ ,

because _____ .

I felt _____ ,

because _____ .

Rerate your mood. Now that you've completed this portion of the exercise, rate your mood again here on the scale from 1 to 10: _____. How do you account for any changes?

_____

_____

_____

Tuesday

Rate your mood. Before starting this part of the exercise, rate your mood on a scale from 1 to 10, with 1 meaning "miserable" and 10 meaning "good." Put your rating here: _____.

I felt _____,

because _____.

I felt _____,

because _____.

I felt _____,

because _____.

I felt _____,

because _____.

I felt _____,

because _____.

Rerate your mood. Now that you've completed the exercise, rate your mood here on the scale from 1 to 10: _____. How do you account for any changes?

_____

_____

_____

Wednesday

Rate your mood. Before starting this part of the exercise, rate your mood on a scale from 1 to 10, in which 1 means "miserable" and 10 means "good." Put your rating here: _____ .

I felt _____ ,

because _____ .

I felt _____ ,

because _____ .

I felt _____ ,

because _____ .

I felt _____ ,

because _____ .

I felt _____ ,

because _____ .

Rerate your mood. Now that you've completed this part of the exercise, rate your mood again here on the scale from 1 to 10: _____ . How do you account for any changes?

_____

_____

_____

Thursday

Rate your mood. Before starting the next part of the exercise, rate your mood on a scale from 1 to 10, in which 1 means "miserable" and 10 means "good." Put your rating here: _____ .

I felt _____ ,

because _____ .

I felt _____ ,

because _____ .

I felt _____ ,

because _____ .

I felt _____ ,

because _____ .

I felt _____ ,

because _____ .

Rerate your mood. Now that you've completed this part of the exercise, rate your mood again here on the scale from 1 to 10: _____ . How do you account for any changes?

_____

_____

_____

Friday

Rate your mood. Before starting this part of the exercise, rate your mood on a scale from 1 to 10, in which 1 means "miserable" and 10 means "good." Put your rating here: _____ .

I felt _____ ,

because _____ .

I felt _____ ,

because _____ .

I felt _____ ,

because _____ .

I felt _____ ,

because _____ .

I felt _____ ,

because _____ .

Rerate your mood. Now that you've completed this part of the exercise, rate your mood here again on the scale from 1 to 10: _____ . How do you account for any changes?

_____

_____

_____

Saturday

Rate your mood. Before starting the next part of the exercise, rate your mood on a scale from 1 to 10, in which 1 means "miserable" and 10 means "good." Put your rating here: _____ .

I felt _____ ,

because _____ .

I felt _____ ,

because _____ .

I felt _____ ,

because _____ .

I felt _____ ,

because _____ .

I felt _____ ,

because _____ .

Rerate your mood. Now that you've completed this part of the exercise, rate your mood again here on the scale from 1 to 10: _____ . How do you account for any changes?

_____

_____

_____

Sunday

Rate your mood. Before starting the next part of the exercise, rate your mood on a scale from 1 to 10, in which 1 means "miserable" and 10 means "good." Put your rating here: _____ .

I felt _____ ,

because _____ .

I felt _____ ,

because _____ .

I felt _____ ,

because _____ .

I felt _____ ,

because _____ .

I felt _____ ,

because _____ .

Rerate your mood. Now that you've completed this part of exercise, rate your mood here again on the scale from 1 to 10: _____ . How do you account for any changes?

_____

_____

_____

INVESTIGATING EXCEPTIONS

Now that you've focused on "exceptions," times when you feel even a little better, you can explore in more depth to find out what you've done and the resources you've drawn upon to make these good feelings—even the most fleeting ones—happen. The following chart offers a way to elaborate on these exceptions by posing the investigative questions who, what, where, and when (Bertolino and O'Hanlon 2002; Cade and O'Hanlon 1993; deJong and Berg 2008). You may notice that no "why" questions are asked. "Why" questions often stimulate overanalyzing. Some people who are depressed are very much "in their heads," and this can lead to rumination (worrying a problem to death, and going round and round in the same thought pattern with no resolution). Instead of a "why" question ("Why do I feel so bad?"), use "what" or "how" questions that focus on resources: for example, "What have I done in the past that has helped?" or "How can I help myself feel better?" (Christensen, Todahl, and Barrett 1999).

Observe how Kelly filled out her chart, then complete the blank one that follows.

Rate your mood. Before starting the next exercise, rate your mood on a scale from 1 to 10, in which 1 means "miserable" and 10 means "good": _____ .

KELLY'S SOLUTIONS

Question	Solution
When? • What's the typical timing (time of day, week, month, or year) when you feel better? • How often do you experience exceptions to depression (once an hour, once a day, once a week)? • How long do they last?	• I feel better at nighttime, so I stay up late to take advantage of this time. • I do better when the weather's warmer and the days are long. • I do better when I have my time structured with social activities. • When I have social activities, I generally feel better for the time I'm with somebody and for several hours afterward.
Where? • Where are you when you feel best? • What is it about the setting that helps you feel better?	• I like to be outdoors. • Forests and water offer comfort and peace. I enjoy exercising outdoors.
What? • What bodily reactions have you experienced when you've felt better? • What actions do you take to make the exception happen? • What do you tell yourself when this happens?	• I'm energetic. There's a lightness in my chest, and my head is clear. • Usually, taking any proactive action helps me—calling friends or family, going out, exercising—or distracting myself (playing sports, or getting involved in a good movie or book). • I tell myself, "See, I don't feel bad all the time. There are some things I can do to make myself feel better."
Who? • Who contributes to your feeling better? • What do they do that helps?	• Generally, I feel better when I'm in any small social gathering. • When I'm with other people, I can forget about myself and concentrate on the other person, what we're doing, and so forth. • Other people help me when they listen to what I have to say.

EXERCISE: Investigate Your Exceptions

In answering these questions, you can either concentrate on a specific situation you named in the previous exercise, or you can consider a period of time when you felt better for a while (you didn't have any depressive symptoms) or felt a bit better (not as many symptoms).

Question	Solution
When? • What's the typical timing (time of day, week, month, or year) when you feel better? • How often do you experience exceptions to depression (once an hour, once a day, once a week)? • How long do they last?	
Where? • Where are you when you feel best? • What is it about the setting that helps you feel better?	
What? • What bodily reactions have you experienced when you've felt better? • What actions do you take to make the exception happen? • What do you tell yourself when this happens?	
Who? • Who contributes to your feeling better? • What do they do that helps?	

Rerate your mood. Now that you've completed the exercise, rate your mood again here on a scale from 1 to 10: _____ . How do you account for any changes?

_____

_____

_____

_____

PUTTING IT ALL TOGETHER

In this chapter, you've spent time identifying times when you felt better, both brief periods and longer periods in which the depression receded. Gather together all the strategies you named in the various exercises in this chapter to make the exceptions occur.

1. What kinds of statements do you tend to make to yourself when you feel better?

_____

_____

_____

_____

2. What kinds of activities do you do when these exceptions to depression occur?

_____

_____

_____

_____

3. Who are you with? What do you say to that person, or how do you interact with him or her?

_____

_____

_____

_____

_____

4.   What personal qualities do you draw upon when you experience these exceptions?

_____

_____

_____

_____

5.   What are some other physical and environmental resources that have helped you feel better in the past?

_____

_____

_____

_____

6.   What are some spiritual and religious resources that have helped you feel better in the past?

_____

_____

_____

_____

CONCLUSION

This chapter has helped you focus on the times when you feel better, which hopefully has led you to see that you're not defined by your depression. "Exception finding" helps you overcome the negative bias depression creates in your thinking. In this chapter, you delved into the circumstances and personal resources you bring that create these "exceptions to depression." By understanding what goes into these "exceptions," you can use the strategies to more consciously overcome your depression.

PART II

Building Motivation

CHAPTER 5

Learning How to Motivate Yourself to Beat Depression

Common symptoms of depression are listlessness and apathy. "What's the point? What's the use?" are the refrain of the depressed person. People with depression typically have very low motivation to take action, which may include low motivation to do the exercises in this workbook. This chapter will delve into ways you can motivate yourself to help yourself feel better, whether by doing the exercises in this workbook to change your patterns, using some of the strengths and resources you identified in previous chapters, working with a therapist, or getting help in some other way. Later, in chapter 6 I'll help you find the motivation it takes to stop any unhealthy coping behaviors.

Much of the material in this chapter is drawn from motivational interviewing (Miller and Rollnick 2002). Originally developed for people with substance-use disorders, it has been adapted for many other uses now, including psychological problems such as depression (Arkowitz, Westra, Miller, and Rollnick 2008). The fundamental principle of motivational interviewing is that when faced with any type of change, people feel ambivalence. In other words, there's a side of you that wants to change, and there's a side of you that doesn't. Motivational interviewing techniques work to address both sides of the ambivalence and tip the scales in favor of making change.

Rate your level of motivation. Before starting to weigh the advantages and disadvantages of changing, as well as those of depression, rate your motivation to take action against your depression. Actions could include, for instance, doing exercises in this workbook, implementing your coping plan (chapter 2), or using one of the tasks you identified in chapter 3 in the scaling questions as something that would get you closer to your goal. On the scale, 10 means "very motivated," and 1 means "not motivated at all": _____ .

DISADVANTAGES OF CHANGING

Before making any type of change, you have to weigh the costs and benefits of making the effort (Miller and Rollnick 2002). What are some reasons *not* to change, *not* to go about anything differently? You might be surprised at this line of questioning. Most likely you've heard from others in your life (and you may have also berated yourself) about what you should be doing. You may feel worse about yourself because you know you "should" be doing something differently than you are but can't seem to find the energy or the motivation. Here you'll look at the costs of changing, because they may be exerting a strong influence on you to take no action. See if you can relate to any of the following reasons for not taking action to change:

Too much effort: Let's acknowledge that it does take effort to make changes and take action. As Barbara says, "It all just feels like too much work. It's so much easier to sleep until eleven, and stay in all day and watch TV, not even bothering to get dressed." It might feel easier not to do anything, especially with the lack of energy that often accompanies depression. Plus, there's no guarantee that you'll feel better. What if you try, but nothing changes? You may feel even more discouraged.

Fear of change: This may come in different forms, but basically dealing with depression sometimes means you'll have to change certain ways of behaving that you've had for a long time. Even though certain patterns may not work for you, at least they're familiar. A more specific form of fear of change concerns dealing with some of the underlying reasons for depression. For instance, if you have marital problems you've ignored, what will it mean if you do examine these issues? You may wonder, "What if my changing means I'll have to get divorced?"

Facing that you have depression (Murphy 2008): To work on your depression, you have to acknowledge, at least to some extent, that you're depressed. Many people have myths about depression, such as the following:

- "Being depressed means I'm weak."

- "Being depressed means I'm crazy."

- "Being depressed means I'll be locked up."

- "Being depressed means I'm like _____ [someone in the family with a mental health problem]."

- "I should be able to 'snap out of this.'"

- "I should be able to do this on my own, without getting any help."

- "It's normal for _____ [elderly people, women in menopause, someone dealing with a breakup] to be depressed."

Fear of pain: You may be afraid you'll feel even more pain if you try to deal with your depression. What if it hurts to look at some of the things that have contributed to your depression? You may believe it's easier to try to ignore these things and trudge on with your life. You may fear that if you take the time to focus on your symptoms, you'll feel overwhelmed by your pain. You may have very specific concerns, such as these: "What if I start crying and never stop?" "What if I lose control?" Or you may tell yourself, "I don't want to dig up things from the past."

It's important to address any reasons you have for not wanting to change, because they can be powerful forces against trying to do anything differently. The following chart takes the disadvantages of changing offered previously and rebuts them, point by point.

ARGUING AGAINST AVOIDING CHANGE

Reason Not to Address Depression	Rebuttal
Too much effort	- Doing nothing feeds into depression. - If you do nothing, you'll get nothing, while energy begets energy (the law of inertia takes hold: a body at rest stays at rest, while a body in motion stays in motion). - Structure (having things to do) is a good way to combat depression.
Fear of change	- You can validate for yourself that change is scary; however, you can also ask, "How well is what I'm doing working for me?"

Fear of being weak	• It takes a lot of courage to admit and face a problem. • Depression doesn't arise from personal weakness but, rather, a confluence of other factors (genetics and environmental factors working together).
Fear of being considered crazy	• Depression is a treatable clinical condition. • Depression has a lifetime prevalence of 16 percent (Kessler et al. 2003); that many people in the United States can't be considered "crazy." • Consider the number of historical figures who've had depression, including Abraham Lincoln and Winston Churchill. Do you consider them "crazy"?
I should be able to "snap out of this" or pull myself out of it.	• Willpower won't relieve a person's depression; you can't just decide not to be depressed.
It's normal for someone like me to be depressed.	• Depression is a treatable clinical condition.
I'll feel even more pain if I try to deal with my depression.	• Depression is very painful and can continue if not addressed; if you deal with what's bothering you, there'll be an end to the pain.
What if I start crying and never stop? What if I lose control?	• Crying is a healthy response to sadness and stress; the feelings will naturally dissipate. No one has cried forever.
I don't want to dig up things from the past.	• The approach taken in this workbook isn't about "digging up things from the past." It's more oriented in the present and in identifying and using your strengths.
What if I try and fail?	• If you don't take the risk of trying, you won't succeed; you can take small, safe steps toward change (which is what this workbook purports).

Which reasons for avoiding addressing depression apply to you? Can you think of other reasons why you don't want to make the effort to change?

_____

_____

_____

_____

Rerate your motivation level. After having explored reasons not to change and rebutting them, where are you now on the motivation scale from 1 to 10? _____ How did the rating change? What do you think contributed to any change?

_____

_____

_____

_____

Rate your motivation level. If you're moving on to the following section right after completing the previous one, then there's no need to rate your motivation again. However, if you're reading on at a different time, please rate your current level of motivation here: _____ .

ADVANTAGES OF BEING DEPRESSED

Another way to look at lack of motivation to change is to ask yourself, "Am I getting anything out of feeling depressed?" Although your first thought might be, "I feel so awful when I'm depressed; there can't possibly be any benefits," many people derive what's called *secondary gains* from their problems.

Following are some common reasons why people may choose (consciously or unconsciously) to continue with habits, behaviors, or thought patterns that ensure they'll remain depressed:

- "I can blame other people for how I feel and not have to do anything to help myself. What would other people expect of me if I didn't have depression? What if changing means that people won't take care of me anymore?"

  For some people, depression may be a way of abdicating responsibility. For example, Barbara was angry at others for not helping her feel better or keeping her company. She didn't believe she should have to do something to create a life for herself after her husband died six years earlier.

- "I can punish people in my life." Kelly, a twenty-seven-year-old woman, realized that by being depressed and miserable, she was punishing her parents for how they'd treated her when she was growing up. By being depressed, she was, in effect, telling them how bad a job they'd done. If she felt better, she believed she was "letting them off the hook." Of course, the person she was punishing the most was herself.

  Barbara was unwilling to try to do things for herself, because she believed her daughter Petra and her family should move back to the city where Barbara lived in order to take care of her. After all, all her friends' children had eventually moved back; why couldn't Petra? If Barbara started doing things for herself, it would let Petra "off the hook." Instead, Barbara liked to call Petra every day to tell her how bad she felt to let Petra know "what she was doing to me."

- "I won't be 'deep' and 'unique' anymore." Some people believe that if they were happier, it would mean they would be shallow or "like everyone else."

- "I won't be creative anymore." Some artistic types believe that their depression fuels their creativity, and without it, they might not be inspired to write, paint, and so forth.

- "Who would I be without the depression? It's my personality to be negative and pessimistic." Such wonderings may be yours if you have identity concerns, especially if depression has been with you for a long time. I've heard people with long-standing depression say, "This is who I am."

- "My relationships might change." Perhaps all your friends are depressed, or at least cynical, pessimistic, and negative. Maybe you wonder what you'd talk about to friends if you weren't complaining about how bad things are.

- "I'd have to work or do other things I don't want to do." For example, Peter, in addition to being depressed, has been diagnosed with PTSD. He realizes that if he heals from this disorder, he'll have to return to work, which he's reluctant to do.

ARGUING AGAINST STAYING DEPRESSED

Reason to Stay Depressed	Rebuttal
Other people have to take care of me.	• Other people tend to be resentful when they're manipulated into a caregiving role. • There are also some existential realities involved in human existence (Yalom and Leszcz 2005), such as finding meaning and recognizing that life is unfair at times, that we all die eventually, and that regardless of how much help we receive from others, we alone are responsible for the way we live our lives.
Depression makes me "deep."	• People can be complex and unique without being depressed.
I'll lose my creativity without depression.	• Usually the symptoms of depression—apathy, fatigue, a sense of meaninglessness and hopelessness—do not lead to creativity in particular or productivity in general.
Who will I be without depression?	• Consider exploring different behaviors rather than a personality overhaul.
What will my friends and I talk about if we don't complain about how bad everything is?	• Endlessly talking about the problem only reinforces the depression. There are lots of other healthy topics to discuss: the interesting things that are going on, the productive things you're doing, the relationships that are flourishing, the goals you're pursuing, and how you're working to surmount life challenges.

Who will my friends be?	• It's true that "birds of a feather flock together." You may indeed have a depressed circle of friends. But as you start to beat your depression, you owe it to yourself to surround yourself with positive, hopeful, and energetic people who are working to deal with life's challenges. If you don't know where to find these people, you may discover that as you feel less depressed, you'll start meeting new people. But you can also meet them through organizations that are focused on growth or healthy pursuits, such as religious organizations, gyms, clubs, continuing-education classes, 12-step groups, and so forth.

Perhaps none of the reasons discussed so far seems to fit you, so here's an opportunity to explore other possible explanations. Ask yourself: what makes you think you should keep things the way they are (Westra and Dozois 2008)?

_____

_____

_____

_____

Sometimes people are able to unearth the reasons for "staying the same" by writing a letter to the "depression" as if it were a friend. This technique was originally formulated by Treasure and Schmidt (2008) for eating disorders but it can be used for depression, as well. (Later, you can do another version of this exercise in which you address depression as an enemy.) An example from Zoe, a twenty-seven-year-old woman, shows how this is done:

Dear Depression:

You protect me from feeling too overwhelmed by life and its demands. When it gets to be too much and I feel the stress, you just shut me down so that I don't have to feel anything. You help me feel that I'm sensitive. My mother always said I was bad and cared about no one, but because I hurt, it tells me that she's not right about me. My mother would be happy that I'm depressed, because it means I care, maybe too much.

Thanks for always being there,

Zoe

In this letter, you can see that depression seems to protect Zoe from having to deal with stress and some of life's demands. The depression also appears to "prove" something to her mother about Zoe's worth as a person. These are important reasons for Zoe to acknowledge, because they could be holding her back from moving out of her depression. Sometimes insight into these reasons will start to dissipate their power. In other cases, there may be a need to do more work on certain beliefs, such as Zoe's reasoning that "depression means I'm a worthwhile person." (See chapter 8 for more information on working with this type of belief.)

Rerate your motivation level. After having explored the reasons to keep depression around, where are you now on the motivation scale from 1 to 10? _____ How did the rating change? What do you think contributed to any change?

_____

_____

_____

_____

Rate your motivation level. If you're moving on to the next section right after completing the previous one, then there's no need to rate your motivation again. However, if you're reading on at a different time, please rate your current level of motivation here: _____ .

DISADVANTAGES OF DEPRESSION

In this section, you'll explore why it's a good idea to take action to defeat your depression. Besides its debilitating pain, depression may impair many aspects of your life, which we'll discuss next.

Partner Problems

Depressed people often have marital problems. Because of their symptoms (low energy, apathy, lack of enjoyment, hopelessness), depressed people aren't fun to be around. They're negative in general and may be critical toward their partners. They may also frustrate their partners' attempts to help them.

Can you provide an example of when your depression negatively affected your partner?

_____

_____

_____

_____

Other Social Relationships

Apart from children and partners, depression may affect other social relationships. Often people who feel depressed tend to withdraw and limit their social contacts, thereby cutting themselves off from this important avenue to feel better. For example, Barbara complained that her old friends didn't phone anymore, but she also acknowledged that sometimes she wouldn't answer the phone when people called because she "didn't feel like talking." After a while, they stopped calling, since she didn't reciprocate.

Another way that depression can affect social relationships is that depression may not attract other people. Rob often wondered why he didn't have the same number of friends he used to have. He saw it as disloyalty, that all his friends had abandoned him. But he was so cynical about his life and resistant to loved ones' suggestions for how he could make his life better that he frustrated their attempts to help him. He ended up driving them off.

Can you describe how depression has negatively affected your own social relationships?

_____

_____

Physical Health

Depression can be harmful to your physical health: depressed people don't move around and exercise as much as people who aren't depressed do; depressed people are more prone to illness and actually have a higher likelihood of dying earlier (Rugulies 2002). If you're already sick, untreated depression can hurt your chances of recovery.

Shawn said that she got drunk when she felt depressed, and the hangovers the next day were very debilitating. She wondered what kind of effect this would have on her body as she got older. Barbara tended to overeat, and because she often stayed in bed when she was depressed, she was overweight and had suffered a heart attack.

Can you name a specific example of how depression has affected your physical health?

_____

_____

_____

Parenting

Depression in parents can be very harmful to children (Pilowsky et al. 2006). By the time a child with a depressed parent reaches age twenty, there's a 40 percent chance that he or she will have suffered from depression (Beardslee, Versage, and Gladstone 1998). Many possible reasons may account for this trend. Along with genetic factors, parents may be emotionally uninvolved or unavailable, and feel a sense of helplessness in the midst of parenting challenges (Goodman and Gotlib 1999). Parents may inadvertently teach their children to be depressed through showing certain depressive behaviors and thinking, which children may then adopt. Depressed parents also tend to see their children's behavior in a negative light and therefore punish more. If you're a parent and you're unmotivated to help yourself, you might consider benefiting your children as a means to inspire yourself to be more motivated. By paying attention to yourself, you'll help them immeasurably.

With great sadness, Talia said that when she felt depressed, her children constantly asked her, "Are you mad at me?" interpreting her solemn facial expression and low energy as anger at them. She felt bad about this, because she didn't want them to personalize the way she felt.

Can you provide an example of when depression negatively affected your children?

_____

_____

_____

_____

Other Disadvantages of Having Depression

Recall the letter-writing exercise earlier. Now's the time to write a letter to your depression from the perspective of its being an enemy (Treasure and Schmidt 2008). Zoe wrote the following:

Dear Depression:

I'm sick of feeling your pain and how you make me feel that life isn't worth living. You tell me a lie every day, and I don't want to believe you anymore. Your blackness is clogging my head and smothering the life out of me. I don't want you around anymore.

Good-bye,

Zoe

From this letter, Zoe identified that the main disadvantages of depression for her were the pain involved and the feelings of wanting to hurt herself.

Write your letter here:

Dear Depression:

1.   What has your letter told you about the toll depression takes on you?

_____

_____

_____

_____

2.   How has the depression prevented you from living your life the way you want to? (Miller and Rollnick 2002)

_____

_____

_____

_____

3.   Thinking about the future, if you don't do anything about the depression, what do you imagine your life will look like? (Miller and Rollnick 2002)

_____

_____

_____

_____

Rerate your motivation level. After having explored the problems with having depression, where are you now on the motivation scale from 1 to 10? _____ How did the rating change? What do you think contributed to any change?

_____

_____

_____

_____

Rate your motivation level. If you're moving on to the next section right after completing the previous one, then there's no need to rate your motivation level again. However, if you're reading on at a different time, please rate your level of motivation here: _____.

ADVANTAGES OF CHANGING

Recall the exercise in chapter 3 on imagining the future without depression, and then answer the following questions.

1. What do you see yourself being able to do without the depression that you're not doing now? (Miller and Rollnick 2002)

    _____

    _____

    _____

    _____

2. From working on the activities in this chapter and the previous one, what reasons are there for doing something about the depression? (Miller and Rollnick 2002)

    _____

    _____

    _____

    _____

3. Consider a time when you made a major change or quit a habit that bothered you. Was it leaving a relationship, moving, changing jobs, getting a degree, going back to school? How were you able to do that? (Miller and Rollnick 2002)

    a. Write down what you said to yourself that helped you.

    _____

    _____

    _____

b. What were the actions you took?

_____

_____

_____

c. What kind of help did you seek in this situation?

_____

_____

_____

d. What financial or other types of physical resources did you draw upon to get through?

_____

_____

_____

e. What spiritual resources did you draw upon to help with this situation?

_____

_____

_____

f. What personal qualities did you draw upon in this situation?

_____

_____

_____

g. What would others say about what you did?

_____

_____

_____

4. What has this exercise told you about what you can do to apply some of these same strategies to tackling your depression?

_____

_____

_____

_____

Rerate your motivation level. After having explored the advantages of working on the depression, where are you now on the motivation scale from 1 to 10? _____ How did the rating change? What do you think contributed to any change?

_____

_____

_____

_____

Rate your motivation level. If you're moving on to the next section right after completing the previous one, then there's no need to rate your motivation again. However, if you're reading on at a different time, please complete the motivation rating here: _____.

PUTTING IT ALL TOGETHER

Now you'll put together all the work you've done in this chapter in what Miller and Rollnick (2002) refer to as a decisional balance, in which the pros and cons of the depression and the pros and cons of changing are outlined. First, count up the number of items you listed in the sections on the disadvantages of changing and then the number of items for the advantages of changing, and put those numbers here.

Number of disadvantages of changing:

Number of advantages of changing:

When you review the reasons and see the numbers, which side is more heavily weighted? What do you think you need to do to increase your motivation level?

_____

_____

_____

_____

Next, count up the numbers from the sections on the advantages of depression and the disadvantages of depression, and put them here:

Number of advantages of depression:

Number of disadvantages of depression:

When you review the reasons and see the numbers, is it better to stay depressed for the time being or to make changes in order to heal from your depression? What do you think you need to do to feel better?

_____

_____

_____

_____

Rerate your motivation level. After putting all your work together and examining it, where are you now on the motivation scale from 1 to 10? _____ How did the rating change? What do you think contributed to any change?

_____

_____

_____

_____

CONCLUSION

This may have been a difficult chapter to get through, because you may have faced some possible reasons that keep your depression in play. At the same time, developing more awareness of these factors may have dissipated some of their power over you, and you may be in a better place to take action. In this process, you may have identified some beliefs (for example, "I shouldn't have to take responsibility for my life") that you can work on further in chapter 8. For now, the next chapter will continue with motivational interviewing, this time to address any unhealthy coping mechanisms you've used to manage your depression.

CHAPTER 6

Unhealthy Coping Mechanisms

This chapter can help if you've fallen into unhealthy ways of dealing with your depression. It's easy to do, because the pain of depression may make you do whatever you can to escape its effects. Some of these negative coping methods might have emerged in chapter 2, when you explored how you deal with your depression.

How do you know if a coping method is unhealthy or simply neutral? Some activities may be okay to do very seldom or in moderation, but in excess they may become problematic. Examples of such activities include drinking alcohol, watching TV, or playing video games. Other behaviors, such as hard drug use, risky sexual behavior, cutting yourself, or other self-injurious behavior, may present a higher risk of keeping you depressed.

One salient behavior for those who have depression is taking medication. Perhaps you visited a doctor who prescribed medication for depression, and you're uncertain about taking it. Or you're already on medication but thinking of stopping. Medication noncompliance (in other words, not taking your medication regularly if it has been prescribed to you) can be seen as a problem behavior. However, your question might be, "Do I need antidepressant medication to help me feel better?" According to recent evidence, about 50 percent of people respond to an initial antidepressant medication, although that also means that 50 percent do not (Trivedi et al. 2006). When people switch medications (Rush, Trivedi, Wisniewski et al. 2006) or add another medication (Trivedi et al. 2006), this can increase rates of improvement. Sometimes, therefore, it takes a while to determine the best medication(s) for you, so you may need to give it time and work with a doctor closely to find benefits. After giving a medication a chance, you may or may not find it helpful for its influence on your mood, considering its side effects. Later in this chapter, you can analyze the costs and benefits of taking medication to decide for yourself if sticking with medication is what you should be doing. One note of caution is that you must consult your physician if you think you want to stop any medication you've been taking.

EXERCISE: Explore Any Possible Problem Behaviors

Choose a behavior that you're not certain represents a problem but that you're willing to look at further. Write down the behavior here: _____. Now answer yes or no to the following questions. The more yes responses you mark, the more of a problem the behavior might be.

1. Do you feel bad or guilty after you do it? _____

2. Do you have physical problems stemming from the behavior (such as hangovers or weight gain)? _____

3. Do loved ones express concerns over the behavior? _____

4. Do you hide the behavior? _____

5. Are you aware that the behavior causes you to miss out on things that are important to you, such as time with your partner or children? _____

6. Do you ever tell yourself you'll never do it again, but you always seem to do it anyway? _____

7. Does the behavior negatively affect your work or social life? _____

    After considering these questions, what do you think of the behavior? Do you think it's a problem?

_____

_____

_____

_____

If you have more than one unhealthy coping mechanism, choose the one that's giving you the most problems or the one that you're most motivated to change in the next exercise.

ADVANTAGES OF THE PROBLEM BEHAVIOR

Miller and Rollnick (2002) have devised a series of what they call "evocative questions" to consider some of the advantages and disadvantages of changing that they have used for substance use, and that I will translate for depression here. Let's start with the advantages of the problem behavior. In other words, what do you get out of it? This question may come as a surprise, as you may already have been berating yourself for the behavior. But your behavior must be working for you in some way; otherwise you wouldn't do it.

Selma named the following advantages of her TV watching:

- "It distracts me from how bad I feel."

- "I can't think of anything better to do."

- "I'm alone, so the sound of the TV keeps me company."

- "It fills in time in the evenings and weekends."

Louis, thirty-two, said that marijuana was the only thing that helped him feel any better when he was depressed.

- "It changes my perspective and sends my thinking in a more positive direction."

- "It numbs my depression."

- "It helps me focus on tasks I need to get done, like keeping my apartment clean."

- "It helps me feel less lonely."

- "I feel insulated: nothing bothers me; nothing can touch me."

Tina said that she stayed with her abusive husband because she felt hopeless about making it on her own. She listed the various advantages to being in the relationship as follows:

- "I get some companionship, even though much of it's unpleasant."

- "I have financial support, since my husband has a job."

- "My children have a father who lives with them."

- "After the abuse, my husband says he's sorry and acts nice to me."

- "At times, he says he'll change, and I'd like to believe he will."

- "I have a place to live as long as I stay with him."

- "My religion says I can't divorce, so I feel like I'm being a good Catholic by staying with him."

Snyder was considering stopping taking his antidepressant medication, because the only advantage that he could name was that he was less anxious. Because he wasn't able to see any more advantages, he asked a couple of close friends how they saw him on medication compared to when he was off it. This is a good idea, because often, others may see us more realistically than we see ourselves. As a result of the ensuing conversations, Snyder added other advantages of taking medication to his list:

- "I'm no longer afraid to travel [before, his anxiety had precluded travel, but when on medication, he'd made a cross-country trip]."

- "I've become willing to consider having a relationship [before starting medication, he was always cynical about the possibility of relationships]."

Rate your motivation level. In line with the emphasis in this part of the book, you'll be asked to rate the extent to which you're motivated to change the problem behavior. On the scale, 10 means "very motivated," and 1 means "not motivated at all." Put your rating here: _____.

EXERCISE: Explore the Advantages of the Problem Behavior

Write here all the advantages of your problem behavior. What does it do for you?

1.   Does your problematic behavior protect you from the pain of depression?

_____

_____

_____

_____

2.   Does the behavior help you deal with stress?

_____

_____

_____

_____

3.   Does your problematic behavior help you reach your goals (for example, you use amphet-
      amines so you can work harder)?

_____

_____

_____

_____

4.   Does your problematic behavior help you get along with other people better (for example,
      give you the courage to socialize in bars)?

_____

_____

_____

_____

5.   Can you think of other purposes that the problem behavior serves?

_____

_____

_____

_____

Rerate your motivation level. Where are you now on the motivation scale from 1 to 10?
_____ How did the ratings change? What do you think contributed to any change?

_____

_____

_____

_____

DISADVANTAGES OF THE PROBLEM BEHAVIOR

Along with the advantages of the problem behavior, there may also be disadvantages: the ways your behavior hurts you or others. Certain problem behaviors actually encourage depression to develop. A particular example involves drinking alcohol; although some people get drunk to deal with their depression, alcohol is a depressant. Even people who don't have preexisting depression can develop depression after a period of heavy drinking. Depression can also occur after a person has put up with an abusive or unhealthy relationship for a while. Women who've been in violent relationships are often depressed as a result (Golding 1999).

For Tina, the following were some of the disadvantages of staying in an unhealthy relationship:

- "I get physically hurt."

- "I feel depressed about the situation."

- "My children see the violence, and it can't be good for them."

- "My children hit me, because they see my husband hitting me."

- "When they grow up, my children might become abusers or victims."

- "I don't have any friends, because my husband doesn't let me see anyone and I'm embarrassed for anyone to know what I have to live with."

Selma described the disadvantages of her TV watching:

- "I've gained weight from being physically inactive and snacking while watching TV."

- "I feel guilty, because I should be doing something worthwhile."

- "I don't even like the programs."

Louis listed the problems associated with his marijuana smoking:

- "I have to keep smoking more and more to get the same 'high.'"

- "When I have marijuana on hand, I smoke it all day, not just when I feel bad."

- "When I run out of marijuana, it's hard to get more, and I have to make a lot of phone calls and run around to find someone who has it."

- "When I run out, I have uncomfortable cravings."

- "It's illegal, so there's a chance I could get arrested for a drug-related crime."

- "There's random drug testing at work, so I could get caught."

- "To get marijuana, I have to hang around people I'd be embarrassed for my other friends to see me with."

- "My girlfriend complains that when I'm high, it feels like I'm a 'different person,' and she doesn't want to be around me."

- "When I'm high, I eat a lot of junk food, which can't be good for me."

- "I don't want to be around other people, because I feel paranoid that they know I'm high."

- "I already feel apathetic because I'm depressed, and then the marijuana makes me feel even more apathetic."

Snyder, considering his use of antidepressants, wrote the following disadvantages of continuing the medication:

- "I'm constipated."

- "I don't feel as sexual."

Rate your motivation level. Before beginning the next exercise, how motivated are you now to do something about your problem behavior on a scale from 1 to 10, in which 10 means "very motivated" and 1 means "not motivated at all"? Write your rating here: _____ .

EXERCISE: Explore the Disadvantages of the Problem Behavior

Now consider all the disadvantages of the problem behavior, exploring these areas of your life:

- Physical health

- Relationships

- Employment

- Legal status

- Your feelings about yourself

- Goals for the future

- The values you hold for yourself (for example, being a hard worker, being honest, or valuing relationships)

1. How has the problem behavior prevented you from moving forward in your life? (Miller and Rollnick 2002)

_____

_____

_____

_____

2. Considering the future, if you don't do anything about your problem behavior, what do you imagine things will look like? (Miller and Rollnick 2002)

_____

_____

_____

_____

Rerate your motivation level. Where are you now on the motivation scale from 1 to 10? _____ How did the rating change? What do you think contributed to any change?

_____

_____

_____

_____

DISADVANTAGES OF CHANGING THE PROBLEM BEHAVIOR

In any type of change, you have to weigh the costs and benefits of making the effort. What are some reasons *not* to change, *not* to do anything different? Two major reasons come to mind: First, as discussed in chapter 5, it takes effort to make change. Not only will you have to plan and implement strategies to overcome a habit that's not working for you, but you'll also have to find new ways of coping with your depression. Second, although a behavior may not be working well for you, to some extent it's comfortable and familiar. Stopping the behavior means you'll have to forge new territory; you may have to face your depression and try out new behaviors to manage it.

Rate your motivation level. Before beginning the next exercise, rate how motivated you are now to do something about your problem behavior on a scale from 1 to 10, in which 10 means "very motivated" and 1 means "not motivated at all." Write your rating here: _____ .

EXERCISE: Explore the Disadvantages of Changing the Problem Behavior

1. What kind of effort would go into changing the behavior? What would you have to do?

_____

_____

_____

_____

2. Would you have to change your circle of friends (for example, if they all drink a lot and you're trying to stop drinking)?

_____

_____

_____

_____

3.   Would you have to move (for example, since there was a crack house down the street from her, Marlatta had to move so that the temptation wasn't constantly around her)?

_____

_____

_____

_____

4.   Would you have to change jobs (for example, if you work in a bar or restaurant, you might find that you can't do that type of job without drinking, using drugs, or smoking cigarettes)?

_____

_____

_____

_____

5.   Next, write down the disadvantages of changing your unhealthy behavior. In Barbara's case, it was remaining physically inactive; as a result of her weight, she had diabetes and had suffered a heart attack.

    •   Barbara said it would take too much work; it was much easier to do nothing.

    •   She was worried about feeling physical discomfort while exercising. She said she didn't like the feeling of exerting herself.

_____

_____

_____

_____

Rerate your motivation level. Where are you now on the motivation scale from 1 to 10? _____ How did the rating change? What do you think contributed to any change? *Example:* Snyder originally wanted to stop taking his medication mainly because of the sexual side effects. As he said it, "I don't have much pleasure in my life. Feeling sexual is one of the things I enjoy." However, he saw that he was getting a lot of the advantages of the medication. He decided that he would talk to his doctor about his sexual-side-effect concerns but that he would continue with the medication because of the benefits it gave him.

_____

_____

_____

_____

ADVANTAGES OF CHANGING THE PROBLEM BEHAVIOR

In this section, you'll explore why it's a good idea to take action to stop the problem behavior. Continuing with the example of Tina, following are some reasons for her to leave the relationship:

- "I'll feel better about myself if I leave."

- "I'll be able to focus on taking good care of my kids."

- "I can show my children that I can protect them and myself."

- "I can meet new people and hopefully start to get friends."

As another example, forty-year-old Donna often overate when she felt depressed. When considering losing weight, she named the following advantages:

- "I'd look a lot better."

- "I'd feel better about myself."

- "I could wear clothes that show off my body."

- "I could meet guys and start dating."

- "There'd be less strain on my heart, and I'd decrease the risk of diabetes."

Rate your motivation level. Before beginning the next exercise, rate how motivated you are now to do something about your problem behavior on a scale from 1 to 10, in which 10 means "very motivated" and 1 means "not motivated at all." Write your rating here: _____ .

EXERCISE: Explore the Advantages of Changing the Problem Behavior

Write down the advantages of changing your unhealthy behavior:

_____

_____

_____

_____

Rerate your motivation level. Regarding changing the problem behavior, where are you now on the motivation scale from 1 to 10? _____ How did the rating change? What do you think contributed to any change?

_____

_____

_____

_____

PUTTING IT ALL TOGETHER

Now you'll put together all the work you've done so far in this chapter to find out where you stand in relation to the problem behavior. Reviewing and compiling all the pros and cons of a problem behavior involves the decisional balance technique from motivational interviewing (Miller and Rollnick 2002).

Review and count up the number of things you came up with for the previous exercises:

Number of advantages of problem behavior:

Number of disadvantages of the problem behavior:

Number of advantages for changing the behavior:

If "disadvantages of the behavior" and the "advantages of changing" are the longest lists, then you're in good shape! More than likely, you're ready to start changing the behavior.

If "advantages of the behavior" has the highest number, the problem behavior is meeting many of your needs. In this case, you can work on getting these same needs met in other ways. See the case of Louis in the next section for an example of how to do this. You might need to brainstorm about how you can meet these needs (see chapter 3).

If "disadvantages of the behavior" has the highest number, then you might have to brainstorm (see chapter 3) about how to decrease some of these disadvantages. There also may be some very entrenched belief systems that are putting up barriers (see chapter 8). For example, in Barbara's case, she had some beliefs about "working hard" that came from her parents that she needed to explore in more depth, and she identified this as a substantial barrier.

Rerate your motivation level. Where are you now on the motivation scale from 1 to 10? _____ How did the rating change? What do you think contributed to any change?

_____

_____

_____

_____

FINDING THE TOOLS TO CHANGE

One of the biggest fears about changing is that you won't have another strategy to use instead when you feel depressed. How will you replace the good things the problem behavior gives you? The next few chapters will focus on developing your skills and strategies to help you manage your mood. As you build skills in this area, you may find that they apply to your problem behavior as well as your depression. However, you may need additional tools to deal with a severe problem, such as substance abuse—for example, other workbooks, self-help groups, and treatment programs specifically for this problem.

As for the focus of the remainder of the workbook, using Louis as an example, I'll take each of the advantages he named for his marijuana smoking and show the skills that can act as substitutes.

- It changes his perspective. *Alternative:* Cognitive restructuring (see chapter 8) is a healthy way of changing your perspective.

- It numbs his depression. *Alternatives:* Drugs (and alcohol) act to numb depression temporarily, but they're only a short-term solution. You may insist at this point that sometimes that's what you need: a short-term solution that will help you get through an especially bad stretch. However, there are other ways to cope during a particularly painful period. See chapter 1 to develop a coping plan. Working with feelings is another way to understand, identify, and manage your painful emotional states (see chapter 7).

- It helps him focus on tasks he needs to get done, such as keeping his apartment clean. *Alternative:* See chapter 7 to learn how to structure your time.

- It helps him feel less lonely. *Alternative:* See chapter 9 for information on building communication and social skills.

- "Nothing bothers me; nothing can touch me." *Alternatives:* Cognitive restructuring can help change your perspective and interpretation of events so that you don't feel as vulnerable (see chapter 8). Improving your communication skills can help you deal with problems that may arise in relationships or other social contacts, a major source of stress (see chapter 9).

DRAWING ON PAST SUCCESSES

Both solution-focused and motivational interviewing experts talk about drawing on strategies you have used successfully before (deJong and Berg 2008; Miller and Rollnick 2002). Like most people, you've probably been able to kick a bad habit, such as smoking cigarettes or nail-biting, in the past. Or, maybe there was a period of time when you were able to stop the behavior you're struggling with now. For example, Marlatta, who's currently plagued by severe depression, has reverted to using alcohol and crack cocaine. She stayed sober for eleven months previously by "staying away from my old neighborhood and people on the street." She also had activities, such as helping her niece with her children and holding a job as a janitor, that occupied her time.

Rate your motivation level. Before beginning the following exercise, rate how motivated you are now to do something about your problem behavior on a scale from 1 to 10, in which 10 means "very motivated" and 1 means "not motivated at all." Put your rating here: _____ .

EXERCISE: Recall How You've Overcome
Problem Behaviors

Consider a time when you were able to quit a problem behavior (Miller and Rollnick 2002). Answer the following questions to get in touch with the resources you used to help during that time.

1.   What was it that you stopped doing?

_____

_____

_____

_____

   a.   Write down what you said to yourself that helped you.

_____

_____

_____

   b.   What actions did you take?

_____

_____

_____

   c.   What kind of help did you seek in this situation?

_____

_____

_____

   d.   What financial or physical resources did you draw upon to get through?

_____

_____

_____

e. What spiritual resources did you draw upon to help with this situation?

_____

_____

_____

f. What personal qualities did you draw upon in this situation?

_____

_____

_____

g. What would others say you did successfully to cope with this problem behavior?

_____

_____

_____

2. List the actions you took to cope with the problem behavior:

_____

_____

_____

_____

Rerate your motivation level. Where are you now on the motivation scale from 1 to 10? _____ How did the rating change? What do you think contributed to any change?

_____

_____

_____

_____

CONCLUSION

This chapter has given you the chance to explore any potentially harmful coping methods you've used to manage your depression. The next chapter deals with the role feelings play in depression, and shows how you can recognize your feelings and cope with them in healthy ways. Painful or uncomfortable feelings may underlie the depression. You may have also numbed your feelings, as well as your depression, with the problem behavior that you examined in this chapter. Later chapters will focus on building healthy coping skills to overcome your depression.

PART III

Building Skills

CHAPTER 7

Identifying Your Depression Triggers

In chapter 1, you completed some brief checklists to determine if you might be depressed. In the ensuing chapters, you spent time identifying and bolstering your strengths, as well as building your motivation for tackling your depression. Now you'll do some work to identify the things that happen to start your depression, called *triggers*. I avoid the wording, "cause your depression," because that implies that these incidents were directly responsible for the depression and aren't subject to change. Triggers, in contrast, are more transient and malleable. If you can figure out what yours are, you may be able to prevent your depression or limit its intensity or duration.

Triggers can occur in many aspects of your life:

- Thoughts

- Your internal physical state

- Social events

- The environment that surrounds you

- Feelings

Rate your mood. Rate your mood here on a scale from 1 to 10: _____ .

THINKING PATTERNS

As discussed in the introduction, professionals who treat depression from a cognitive behavioral approach believe that thoughts, attitudes, and beliefs (in other words, the things we tell ourselves) are behind depressed moods. Thinking thoughts such as, "Nothing's going to turn out right," "This always happens," or "There's no hope" could make you feel depressed. Although it's debatable whether thoughts and attitudes are the primary causes of depression, getting control of your thoughts and applying them toward more productive lines of thinking can help prevent depression from sinking in. Even if you're caught up in a depressive episode, you can choose to think, "This is painful, but everyone has these feelings sometimes, and I'm not going to always feel this way. I can handle it, and it'll soon pass. In the meantime, I can deal with it," rather than the opposite: "I can't stand this. This is too painful. It's always going to be this way."

Can you see how the latter set of statements makes the depression dig in deeper, whereas the former recognizes that it's a transient mood state that will change? You'll focus on becoming more aware of your thinking patterns in chapter 8. Given that at this point you may have limited understanding of your thoughts and how they contribute to depression, see if you can identify and write down what you say to yourself that tends to make you feel worse. Here are some common examples:

- "Nothing ever works out for me."

- "If I don't do this perfectly, then I'm a failure."

- "Everyone's better than I am."

Write down your thoughts that contribute to depression:

_____

_____

_____

_____

YOUR PHYSICAL STATE

Some people have health problems that result in their feeling depressed. For instance, Tammy, who has MS, is also depressed. Currently researchers are uncertain about whether biological aspects of MS contribute to depression, but certain medications, such as beta interferon, may cause depression in some people (Arnett and Randolph 2006). From a psychosocial (rather than only a biological perspective), it was easy to see why Tammy's chronic illness would lead to depression. Restrictions in physical mobility and being unable to work made it difficult for her to get around, have social contact, or earn a living. Additionally, physical pain was difficult to manage. Complicating the picture is that depression and psychological stress may worsen a physical problem, such as MS.

Perhaps you have a chronic disability, but even if you don't, there are other minor physical issues that might contribute to depression if you're sensitive to their effects. Some people find that their moods are poor if they don't get enough sleep or work too hard, and don't get enough relaxation time. Others need to keep their blood-sugar levels balanced and eat at regular times; otherwise they start to feel "down" and experience low energy.

There are often ways you can cope with physical issues around your depression. For instance, Tammy was seeing an occupational therapist on a regular basis toward the realistic goal of walking without a cane. Nicole, who has young children who wake up at 6 a.m. each morning, realized that if she didn't get enough sleep, her mood would suffer the next day, so she made a point of going to bed by 11 p.m.

1.   Write about how your physical state plays a role in your becoming depressed.

_____

_____

_____

_____

2.   What can you do about some of these physical issues?

_____

_____

_____

_____

DISAPPOINTING OR PAINFUL SOCIAL EVENTS

In this section we'll explore events that happen in your relationships with other people that contribute to your feeling rejected, left out, or abandoned, as well as when you feel used, exploited, pushed around, or manipulated into doing something you don't want to do. These types of experiences leave many people feeling depressed. Examples include not getting invited to an event that others are going to, exclusion from a conversation, a friend's failure to return your call, someone's rudeness to you, or someone's talking you into doing something you didn't want to do. Later in this workbook, I'll cover working with your thoughts to help you interrupt these events in a realistic way rather than become distraught over them (chapter 8). Chapter 9 will work on communication and social skills so that you can develop some ways to avoid these situations or deal with them better if they arise.

For now, just identify social or interpersonal situations in the past that have led to feelings of depression:

_____

_____

_____

_____

ENVIRONMENTAL SURROUNDINGS

The physical environment, such as barren, dirty, ugly, or colorless surroundings, may lead some people to feel bad. Certain weather, such as gray, rainy, or cold days that lack sunshine, triggers depression in others. There's even a diagnosable form of depression called *seasonal affective disorder* (also called *SAD*) that happens in winter with the shortage of natural light. If you live in a dangerous neighborhood, a constant feeling of being unsafe may contribute to your feeling depressed.

There are some actions you can take to overcome environmental stressors. For instance, you can use a light box to treat seasonal affective disorder. As another example, to reduce the drabness of his office surroundings, Gabe asked his boss if he could use office funds to buy colorful prints to spruce up the walls, which were bare and scuffed. She agreed, and everyone complimented him on how he'd brightened up the office space. Both the recognition of his efforts and the improved environment helped Gabe feel better. Although I'm not claiming in this latter example that depression can be cured with such a relatively simple intervention, it's important to consider making changes in an environment that depresses you. In this way, you'll realize that you have some control over how you feel, and can take action to brighten your surroundings.

1. Name how your physical surroundings play a role in your depression.

_____

_____

_____

_____

2. What can you do to overcome the impact of your environment on your depression?

_____

_____

_____

_____

Rerate your mood. Now that you've completed these sections, rate your mood here on the scale from 1 to 10: _____. How do you account for any changes?

_____

_____

_____

_____

FEELINGS

We'll spend more time on "feelings" than the other triggers, because people who are depressed are often lost under the blanket experience of depression. They may have lost touch with the underlying feelings or have never learned what they were in the first place. Although there are many nuanced words for different feelings, I'll discuss the basic four:

- Anger

- Sadness

- Fear

- Happiness

You may be surprised to learn that all other feelings are variations of these. Anger encompasses frustration, irritation, annoyance, and rage, among other nuances. Sadness involves hurt and loss. Fear encapsulates anxiety, nervousness, and embarrassment. Happiness involves contentment and pleasure, as well as ecstasy.

You might ask, where does boredom fit in? Boredom can be a presage of depression; that is, there are things you can do (or should be doing), but you have no interest in doing anything. Boredom can also be frustration (anger), because you don't have enough to do or you're not stimulated enough.

Where does depression fit in? Depression, as defined here, isn't a feeling but a clinical condition, and at least one of the four main feelings underlies the experience. In the next exercise, you'll learn how to identify these feelings.

Rate your mood. Rate your mood here on the scale from 1 to 10: _____ .

EXERCISE: Identify Your Feelings

The purpose of this exercise is to help you learn about your experience with different feelings, and how they may play into your depression. For each feeling, name three times you regularly experience the feeling in your current life. Examples are included in the exercises to help you start thinking about the feelings. If you have problems doing these exercises, try either of these prompts:

- Since you don't know, just make up something.

- If you weren't feeling depressed, when would you experience this particular feeling?

1. **Sadness:** Peter said he felt sad because he didn't see his daughter more often, since he had to live far away from her. At that point, he stalled and was unable to come up with any other feelings of sadness. When asked to "just make it up," Peter said he was sad that he couldn't turn to his father for help and advice because he was supposed to "be a man and be able to handle it."

   When do you tend to feel sad?

_____

_____

_____

2. **Anger:** Sometimes when people are asked to do the exercise on anger, they start with very impersonal situations, such as complaining about "traffic" or "people who don't wait their turn." However, you'll want to home in on situations that are more personal for you and that involve your immediate circumstances.

   At first Kelly denied that she ever felt angry. When asked to "just make it up," she said she was angry that a man she'd recently met wouldn't "take no for an answer" and kept calling and asking her out. Another man she'd been dating had recently stopped contacting her, seemingly without good reason. She also felt angry because she felt excluded from her coworkers' conversations. She was surprised at the end of creating this list how many things did make her angry.

   One hypothesis of depression is that it's anger "turned inward" on the self, which may be particularly applicable to women, who've traditionally not been taught to express anger. If you find, from doing the exercise, that you have difficulty experiencing anger, you can work on this further in the next exercise, "Focus on a Feeling."

   When do you tend to feel angry?

_____

_____

_____

_____

3. **Fear:** Kelly also said that she didn't feel fear, but when asked again to make it up, she quickly spoke about her fears that she wouldn't do well in her graduate-school program, that people wouldn't like her, and that she'd be all alone.

   When do you tend to feel fear?

_____

_____

_____

_____

From doing the exercise, which feelings do you seldom feel or have difficulty writing about: sadness, fear, or anger? In the example of Kelly, although both anger and fear were difficult for her, anger topped her list of "forbidden" feelings.

Doing this exercise may help you gain awareness of feelings that might unknowingly trigger depression. By unearthing these feelings, allowing yourself to feel them, and dealing with them more effectively, you may find that your depression starts to dissolve.

Sometimes people worry that they'll be unable to cope with certain feelings. For example, people believe that if they let themselves feel sadness, they may start crying and never stop. Or, people believe that if they allow themselves to feel fear, they may be paralyzed and unable to function. A point of reassurance is that the feelings, in the long run, will be much less painful and difficult than the depression you're experiencing now.

Rerate your mood. Now that you've completed this exercise, rate your mood here on the scale from 1 to 10: _____ . How do you account for any changes?

_____

_____

_____

_____

EXERCISE: Focus on a Feeling

As a follow-up to the "Identify Your Feelings" exercise, take a feeling that was difficult for you to feel (say anger or fear), and for the next week, five times a day list when you experienced that feeling. Since you're not used to doing this, tune in to the underlying feeling when you next experience depression. Use particular episodes of depression as a signal to search for that feeling going on. For instance, Kelly said, "I feel angry when my professor tells us she's going to test us on certain material and then bases the exam on other topics. I also feel angry that my advisor doesn't return my calls or e-mails. It feels as if I don't matter to her at all, and that makes me feel sad as well." The purpose of this exercise is to help you start to recognize your feelings and understand the role they play in your depression. Assess the impact of doing this exercise each day on the way you feel.

Monday

Rate your mood. Before starting the following part of the exercise, rate your mood on a scale from 1 to 10, in which 1 means "miserable" and 10 means "good." Put your rating here: _____ .

I feel _____ ,

because _____ .

I feel _____ ,

because _____ .

I feel _____ ,

because _____ .

I feel _____ ,

because _____ .

I feel _____ ,

because _____ .

Rerate your mood. Now that you've completed this part of the exercise, rate your mood here on the scale from 1 to 10: _____ . How do you account for any changes?

_____

_____

_____

Tuesday

Rate your mood. Before starting the next part of the exercise, rate your mood on a scale from 1 to 10, in which 1 means "miserable" and 10 means "good." Put your rating here: _____.

I feel _____,

because _____.

I feel _____,

because _____.

I feel _____,

because _____.

I feel _____,

because _____.

I feel _____,

because _____.

Rerate your mood. Now that you've completed this part of the exercise, rate your mood here on the scale from 1 to 10: _____. How do you account for any changes?

_____

_____

_____

Wednesday

Rate your mood. Before starting the next part of the exercise, rate your mood on a scale from 1 to 10, in which 1 means "miserable" and 10 means "good." Put your rating here: _____ .

I feel _____ ,

because _____ .

I feel _____ ,

because _____ .

I feel _____ ,

because _____ .

I feel _____ ,

because _____ .

I feel _____ ,

because _____ .

Rerate your mood. Now that you've completed this part of the exercise, rate your mood here on the scale from 1 to 10: _____ . How do you account for any changes?

_____

_____

_____

Thursday

Rate your mood. Before starting the next part of the exercise, rate your mood on a scale from 1 to 10, in which 1 means "miserable" and 10 means "good." Put your rating here: _____ .

I feel _____ ,

because _____ .

I feel _____ ,

because _____ .

I feel _____ ,

because _____ .

I feel _____ ,

because _____ .

I feel _____ ,

because _____ .

Rerate your mood. Now that you've completed this part of the exercise, rate your mood here on the scale from 1 to 10: _____ . How do you account for any changes?

_____

_____

_____

_____

Friday

Rate your mood. Before starting the next part of the exercise, rate your mood on a scale from 1 to 10, in which 1 means "miserable" and 10 means "good." Put your rating here: _____ .

I feel _____ ,

because _____ .

I feel _____ ,

because _____ .

I feel _____ ,

because _____ .

I feel _____ ,

because _____ .

I feel _____ ,

because _____ .

Rerate your mood. Now that you've completed this part of the exercise, rate your mood here on the scale from 1 to 10: _____ . How do you account for any changes?

_____

_____

_____

_____

Saturday

Rate your mood. Before starting the next part of the exercise, rate your mood on a scale from 1 to 10, in which 1 means "miserable" and 10 means "good." Put your rating here: _____ .

I feel _____ ,

because _____ .

I feel _____ ,

because _____ .

I feel _____ ,

because _____ .

I feel _____ ,

because _____ .

I feel _____ ,

because _____ .

Rerate your mood. Now that you've completed this part of the exercise, rate your mood here on the scale from 1 to 10: _____ . How do you account for any changes?

_____

_____

_____

_____

Sunday

Rate your mood. Before starting the next part of the exercise, rate your mood on a scale from 1 to 10, in which 1 means "miserable" and 10 means "good." Put your rating here: _____ .

I feel _____ ,

because _____ .

I feel _____ ,

because _____ .

I feel _____ ,

because _____ .

I feel _____ ,

because _____ .

I feel _____ ,

because _____ .

Rerate your mood. Now that you've completed this part of the exercise, rate your mood here on the scale from 1 to 10: _____ . How do you account for any changes?

_____

_____

_____

_____

HANDLING TRIGGERS

Now that you've investigated your triggers for depression, you'll learn ways to handle them in order to prevent depression. Previous sections of the workbook have relied on you to come up with your own answers, which might've led to your feeling more empowered and more hopeful about the future. But you can also choose to learn new ways of acting that have helped other people with their depression. There are many different strategies to prevent depression from taking hold:

- Allow the feelings.

- Manage the feelings.

- Avoid the trigger.

- Change the trigger.

- Cope with the trigger.

- Communicate about the trigger.

Although we're about to explore each of these strategies, upcoming chapters will cover some of the techniques in more depth.

Rate your mood. Before starting the following sections, rate your mood on a scale from 1 to 10, in which 1 means "miserable" and 10 means "good." Put your rating here: _____

Allow the Feelings

Since you've just done some extensive work on feelings, I'll start with how to handle uncomfortable feelings, such as sadness, fear, and anger. One way is to allow the feelings to exist. You may find that your default pattern is to shut down the feelings and perhaps experience depression instead. Alternatively, the next time you have an uncomfortable feeling—either sadness, anger, or fear—allow yourself a few minutes in a quiet and comfortable place, at home, a place of nature or worship, or another safe place, and reflect on the experience of the feeling:

- Where is it in your body or mind?

- What color is it?

- What shape does it have?

- What level of density or intensity does it have?

- What's the sensation like?

- Does the feeling move or change?

Write down your experiences here after you do this activity:

_____

_____

_____

_____

Your feelings may shift from doing this activity, but its main purpose is to allow you to feel unpleasant emotions rather than cover them up with depression. You'll notice that you experience feelings in wavelike patterns. They gain momentum, reach a peak of intensity, and then dissipate until they rise once more. In giving yourself permission to experience the feeling, you'll find that, although it may be painful, its nature is time limited and it may eventually dissipate. At the same time, you'll often need other coping methods to change how you feel.

Manage Your Feelings by Structuring Your Day

The experience of depression can feel overwhelming, as if it could completely take over. A schedule—giving yourself the structure of planned activities—can keep these feelings at a more manageable level. A schedule can also create the sense of meaning that a depressed person often lacks. The second component of managing your feelings on a daily basis is to build in plenty of pleasurable activities.

Structuring your time involves building in obligations (things that you have to get done), working toward your goals, and enjoying pleasurable activities. The reason you need to routinely include pleasurable activities (at least four a day) is that they'll make you feel better. One of the symptoms of depression is experiencing a lack of pleasure and interest in activities. The *thought* of doing something might not be appealing. But when they're in the moment of actually *doing* something potentially fun, relaxing, or engaging, people typically find that they enjoy it more than they thought they would. As a result, their moods are lifted. Here are some common ideas for pleasurable activities, but you're free to come up with your own:

- Exercise

- Watching a favorite television show

- Taking a hot bath or shower

- Calling a friend

- Reading

- Craft work

- Gardening

- Listening to music

- Hanging out with friends

- Going to a restaurant

- Going to a movie

- Watching a movie at home

- Eating a favorite meal or snack

- Window-shopping

Here I'll present a simplified version of the behavioral treatment known as *activity scheduling*, which has been found to work as well as more-complex treatment programs in reducing depression (Cuijpers, van Straten, and Warmerdam 2007). Basically, it involves making a schedule or a to-do list for the day.

A guideline for making a schedule is to first make sure that you break down large tasks into their constituent parts. For instance, rather than "clean house," you can list "clean bathroom," "wash dishes," and "vacuum." Rather than "pay bills," you can list "pay utilities bill," "call electric company about past-due amount," "pay electric bill," "pay credit-card bill," "put checks into envelopes," and "post bills."

Rate your mood. Before you do the next exercise, rate your mood on a scale from 1 to 10: _____ .

EXERCISE: Create a To-Do List

Create a to-do list for the day (or for the next day, depending on when you do this exercise). Include at least four pleasurable activities.

To-Do List:

1.

2.

3.

4.

5.

6.

7.

8.

9.

10.

Rerate your mood. After the day's over and the tasks are completed, rate on a scale from 1 to 10 (in which 10 means "fine") how you feel now: _____ . How does this number differ from your initial rating? How do you account for any changes?

_____

_____

_____

_____

Avoid the Trigger

One strategy for dealing with triggers is to avoid them. For example, you can limit time with a negative friend or coworker who brings you down. Since this example and others like it may require communication and assertiveness skills, these will be covered in chapter 9.

One point to consider here is the extent to which avoidance will work in a particular situation and whether you use it chronically as a way of handling problems. If it's a pessimistic friend who brings you down, the strategy of avoidance works well. However, Peter played video games for hours on end to escape his depression. Mrs. Ayela described that she coped with her abusive husband by avoiding him; she chose to work a lot of hours and then stayed in another room away from him. Although this strategy might work for her on a temporary basis (avoiding an abusive episode), I don't suggest it as a long-term solution to the problem of being married to an abusive partner. One way to determine whether or not avoidance is effective for you is to examine the advantages and disadvantages of the strategy, which was covered in chapter 5.

How do you use avoidance to manage your triggers? How well does this work for you?

_____

_____

_____

_____

Change the Trigger

Another strategy for managing your triggers is to change the circumstances. If you can match the onset of your depression to a particular change in your life that has persisted over time, you may want to see whether you can change that aspect of your life. As an example, let's say that your job, although well paying, brings you down because you work too many hours, it's ill-suited to your personality (for example, it's a sales job that requires extroversion when you're an introvert and would rather be working on your own), or you have to put up with a boss who humiliates you and coworkers you can't get along with. In this case, you could probably do a lot to relieve your feelings of depression by finding a more suitable job and quitting the unpleasant one. This is an extreme example, and oftentimes life circumstances are more of a mix between the good and the bad, but the point is that you can change certain parts of your life. You might consider doing so if your particular circumstances have been persistently depressing over a period of several months.

Of course, there are certain aspects of life that you cannot change. If you develop a chronic illness, you can't change that, although you can work on managing your health and developing other coping skills, which brings you to the next alternative.

How can you change some of the circumstances in your life, if you think they're contributing to your depression? Use the brainstorming process (covered in chapter 3) here to come up with as many ideas as you can.

1. What circumstance needs to be changed?

    _____

    _____

    _____

    _____

2. How might you go about changing this circumstance?

    Idea #1: _____

    Idea #2: _____

    Idea #3: _____

    Idea #4: _____

    Idea #5: _____

    Idea #6: _____

    Idea #7: _____

    Idea #8: _____

    Idea #9: _____

    Idea #10: _____

3. What ideas out of the previous list seem viable?

    _____

    _____

    _____

    _____

Cope with the Trigger

Many different techniques are available for coping with the trigger, although this class of techniques is united by the assumption that you might have no choice but to experience a certain situation (bad weather, job requirements, another person's ingrained personality). Given the inevitability of a particular situation, how can you cope with it as well as you can?

One major technique, mentioned briefly before, is called *cognitive restructuring*, which will be covered in depth in chapter 8. The basic idea here is that what you tell yourself affects the way you feel and act. When people are depressed, they tend to think negatively about themselves, other people, and the situations in their lives. This technique helps you learn how to catch the negative thinking and alter it so that, over time, you improve the way you feel.

Communicate About the Trigger

Communication skills will be covered in depth in chapter 9, so I'll only touch on the topic here. Sometimes depression is triggered because of the way another person has treated you. For example, from doing the previous exercises, Kelly learned that her depression was often triggered by a certain professor in her graduate-school program. He tended to be unclear about requirements for assignments and disapproving about people's responses and performance in class. She decided to speak with him privately about clarifying requirements for assignments and to describe her personal reaction: being afraid to say anything and feeling ill prepared to meet his expectations for class participation.

For now, describe a situation in which a person has triggered you to feel bad. In chapter 9, I'll talk about how to handle it.

_____

_____

_____

_____

CONCLUSION

This chapter has helped you assess in greater detail your experience of depression and what sparks it. Working through the exercises has likely given you a greater sense of control over what happens, so that you can prevent depressive moods, limit their power over you, and help yourself cope with them better.

CHAPTER 8

Working with Your Thoughts and Beliefs

One of the main themes of this workbook has been that you can change the way you feel by altering either your perspective or what you do. In previous chapters, you've changed your perspective by considering your strengths. In this chapter, you'll learn to work with your thoughts more directly through the cognitive behavioral technique, *cognitive restructuring*.

Professionals who come from a cognitive behavioral approach believe that thoughts affect the way you feel, even that thoughts actually *cause* feelings. This workbook takes a less extreme position. A lot of different factors have contributed to your becoming depressed: genetics, hormones, temperament, and stressful life events (see chapter 2). This chapter will address the risk factor of negative thinking (also known as distorted, irrational, unrealistic, or faulty thinking). I'll use the term "unhelpful thinking," because it highlights the purpose here, which is to harness your thoughts in service of solving your depression.

Let's say you feel bad and think, "Nothing works out for me." What's the effect of making such a statement to yourself? It certainly doesn't help you feel any better and will probably make you feel worse. If, instead, you catch this type of thinking and change it, you can impact the way you feel. At this point, you may argue, "But I'm only thinking this way because I feel so bad." In other words, you're saying that your feelings cause your thoughts, but both processes probably operate: your thinking is negative so you become depressed (if other factors are present), and when you're depressed, your thinking becomes even more negative. It's likely a cyclical process, and if you allow yourself to keep thinking this way, you only allow the depression to dig in deeper.

Another reason to pay attention to your thoughts is that when you're depressed, your thinking becomes distorted in a negatively unrealistic way. I know it feels as if your thoughts are "true" and are really what's going on, but when you're depressed, they're often biased when you consider yourself ("I'm no good"), others ("They're out to get me"), and the future ("Nothing's going to change").

HARNESSING THE POWER OF YOUR THOUGHTS

To work on your depressive thinking, three steps are necessary:

1. Identify the unhelpful thoughts.

2. Examine whether they're realistic.

3. Change the thoughts.

Rate your mood. Before starting the following exercise, rate your mood on a scale from 1 to 10, in which 1 means "miserable" and 10 means "good": _____ .

EXERCISE: Identify Unhelpful Thinking

Many people are unaware that they're constantly talking to themselves in their mind, giving themselves continuous messages. This exercise will help you get in touch with the kind of commentary you're giving yourself.

Identify Your Thoughts

One way to identify your thoughts is to check in with them when you start feeling depressed. Kelly identified that she felt worse when she considered breaking up with her boyfriend. When she tuned in to her thoughts, they were: "I'll be all alone. How am I going to make it without him? How will I survive?"

What do you tend to say to yourself either while you're feeling depressed or right before the depression starts? Track this over the next day or so, or whenever you next experience a low mood, and write down at least five thoughts you've identified that seem to contribute to your depressed mood.

Thought #1: _____

Thought #2: _____

Thought #3: _____

Thought #4: _____

Thought #5: _____

Select a thought that gives you the most "emotional charge" or causes you the most harm. This thought can be a continuing focus as you work through the following steps of changing your thinking.

Rerate your mood. Rate on a scale from 1 to 10 (in which 10 means "fine") how you feel now: _____. How does this number differ from your initial rating? How do you account for any changes?

_____

_____

_____

_____

EXAMINE YOUR THOUGHTS

The next step in working with your thoughts after you become aware of them is to examine the extent to which they're helpful. You can try each of these methods, evaluating their effect on your mood.

- Look at the evidence.

- Find a different perspective.

- Use "point-counterpoint."

Look at the Evidence

In this technique, you look at the reality of the situation. The first step is to behaviorally define the supposed disastrous event or the label you've assigned to yourself. Kelly was worried that without her boyfriend, she "wouldn't survive." When asked to deconstruct what this meant, she described that she'd just lie on her apartment floor and be unable to take care of herself. She wouldn't eat or go to work. If she did make it to her job, she'd only cry, embarrassing herself in front of her coworkers.

If you tend to make global negative statements about yourself, such as "I'm stupid" or "There's something wrong with me," you can also break these beliefs down into specific behaviors. For instance, if you believe you're stupid, what type of behaviors do you do that are "stupid"? Mary called herself "stupid," because she was unable to design software and do feats of engineering as did people she knew. She was also absentminded, and tended to misplace her keys and other belongings.

Another way to approach a negative label you've assigned to yourself is to ask, "What do other people do when they're being stupid?" Typically, people who believe they're stupid have different standards of behavior for other people than they have for themselves. When Mary was asked what she saw as stupid in others, she said, "It's when people know better, and they still go ahead and do something, like have an affair with a married man."

Yet another angle is to take a negative global statement, such as "I'm an idiot," and translate this belief into a feared outcome; for example, "What'll happen if I'm an idiot?" An answer could be, "Since I'm an idiot, I won't be able to keep my job, and I'll get fired." As another example, Samantha said, "I'm ugly, and therefore nobody will ever love me, so I'll always be single."

Once you've defined what you mean by your statement, determine whether this is something that could really happen or is true. What tells you that it could happen? For example, what's the evidence that Kelly "can't survive"? Has she ever "not survived" before? She recalled that in previous breakups, she'd lain on her living room floor crying for perhaps two hours at a time at the most. When she'd gone to work, people had been understanding about her emotional state, although she'd cried a couple of times in front of coworkers. Although the feelings of loss were painful during previous breakups, the intensity of the pain wasn't continuous or as all-consuming as she'd previously believed.

When examining her past and how she managed before she met her boyfriend, Kelly realized that she was doing better before she became involved with him. She had a lot of evidence, therefore, that she'd lived alone and "survived" before she met him.

In response to Mary's belief that she was stupid, she recognized she had a bachelor's degree in hotel and restaurant management, and received compliments from friends and family on her cooking ability. After defining what was stupid in others, Mary replied that although she'd done stupid things in her past, she'd never had an affair with a married man, and she had the intelligence to learn from her past mistakes.

If you were to come up with the likelihood that the event will happen or that it's really true, how would you express it as a percentage? For instance, Mrs. Ayela says, "I'm going to be homeless if I divorce my husband." When asked to place a percentage on the likelihood of that actually happening, she admitted that it might be 10 percent. She acknowledged that her job as the office manager of the cleaning company would enable her to pay rent on at least a small apartment. Although she couldn't afford as nice of a house as she presently owned with her husband, she realized that she could make sufficient money to prevent herself from becoming homeless.

With Samantha's belief that she was "ugly," she could examine the evidence of having to be attractive in order to get married. For example, she could go to a place where a lot of people congregated and see whether any "unattractive" people wore wedding rings. Chances are, she'd find that the connection between "being unattractive" and "always single" isn't as highly correlated as she'd previously believed.

Rate your mood. Before starting the next exercise, rate your mood on a scale from 1 to 10, in which 1 means "miserable" and 10 means "good": _____ .

EXERCISE: Where's the Evidence?

Write down the thought you want to examine:

_____

_____

_____

_____

1. Write down the behaviors that make up the belief behind this thought.

    a. For you:

    _____

    _____

    _____

b.   For others:

_____

_____

_____

2.   What will happen if you believe this about yourself?

_____

_____

_____

_____

3.   Given the behaviors you've identified, could this really happen, or is it really true?

_____

_____

_____

_____

4.   What's the likelihood, as a percentage?

_____

_____

_____

_____

5.   What tells you that this could happen, or is true? What evidence do you have?

_____

_____

_____

_____

Rerate your mood. Rate on a scale from 1 to 10 (in which 10 means "fine") how you feel now: _____ . How does this number differ from your initial rating? How do you account for any changes?

_____

_____

_____

_____

Find a Different Perspective

Another way to challenge distorted thinking is to view the problem from another perspective (McKay, Davis, and Fanning 1997): "What's another way of seeing this?" Try to consider a view that gives you credit for the positive aspects of your behavior (Berg 1994), so that you can see yourself in a more benevolent light (Morris, Alexander, and Waldron 1988) or view the "silver lining." A new perspective can sometimes generate new actions in accordance with an altered frame of viewing (Bertolino and O'Hanlon 2002). For instance, if you see yourself as "lazy," it could be that you're "laid back and relaxed, and take things as they come." If you're "boring," you can be thought of as "dependable, steady, consistent, or reliable."

One method to help you find a different perspective is to think of how you'd respond to a specific friend if he or she voiced the negative thought you harbor now. Would you say, "How could you be so stupid? You deserve this." Of course not! You probably wouldn't even say such a thing to your worst enemy, but you may routinely talk to yourself this way.

When Kelly tried to take another perspective, she saw that she might actually feel better if she left her boyfriend, rather than remaining stuck in the belief that she "couldn't survive" without him. Her boyfriend abused drugs and manipulated her emotionally, which made her feel bad about herself and hopeless. When she examined her worst fears and shifted her viewpoint, she realized that if she left him, her mood might actually improve.

As another example, Alison was an artist who often painted when she felt depressed. However, she hadn't received much recognition for her work. She often thought, "I've spent the last twenty years working at my painting, and there's been no use to it at all." One of her friends offered several different viewpoints, or "reframes," of this thought. One reframe was that Alison's art had kept her alive all these years. By being able to externalize her pain through painting, Alison was able to manage her mood, and often experienced satisfaction at capturing her inner experience. A second reframe was that she has remained passionate about her painting, even through periods of depression. Her painting had always given her a sense of purpose.

Rate your mood. Before starting the next exercise, rate your mood on a scale from 1 to 10, in which 1 means "miserable" and 10 means "good": _____ .

EXERCISE: Learn How to Reframe Your Thoughts

1. Take the same thought you worked on in the previous exercise and find an alternative way to see it:

    _____

    _____

    _____

    _____

2. Let's say a person you care about verbalizes the same unhelpful thought as the one you examined previously. How would you respond to that person to help him or her feel better?

    _____

    _____

    _____

    _____

Rerate your mood. Rate on a scale from 1 to 10 (in which 10 means "fine") how you feel now: _____ . How does this number differ from your initial rating? How do you account for any changes?

    _____

    _____

    _____

    _____

Use "Point-Counterpoint"

Recall in chapters 5 and 6 the motivational technique of considering the advantages and disadvantages of your depression, and perhaps a problem behavior. You can use the same technique with unhelpful thoughts, in which you examine the costs and benefits of having the thoughts (Young 1999). This challenges the notion that thoughts are objective reality, that they really exist and are immutable. Considering the advantages and disadvantages of the thoughts can help you become more flexible in your thinking, so that certain entrenched beliefs can start to release their powerful hold.

You might wonder what advantages exist for having dysfunctional thoughts such as, "My life has no meaning." However, there's got to be a payoff; otherwise you wouldn't think that way. One of the main payoffs is that these thought patterns are familiar and safe for you. By believing them, you don't have to consider alternative ways of being or take the risk of trying out new behaviors. A second advantage is that the statements you make to yourself may have been taught by parents and other caregivers when you were young. By believing in these statements, you may have been able to avoid the discomfort of examining these messages for yourself and deciding if they work for you.

Potential disadvantages of these negative thoughts might seem more obvious. Believing that "life has no meaning" will most likely have the impact of ensuring that you won't take risks or challenge yourself to grow. Such thoughts might also justify self-destructive behavior, such as overeating, using alcohol or drugs, or watching too much TV.

Claire decided to work on her thought: "I should be working and getting things done all the time." She found that the advantages of believing this thought were:

- "I'm productive."

- "I'm well regarded at my job."

- "My children and house, and all the other areas of my life, are well taken care of."

- "I experience meaning by accomplishing tasks."

The disadvantages of her belief in this thought were:

- "I don't know how to relax."

- "I experience little pleasure in my life."

- "I'm prone to depression."

- "I have difficulty sleeping through the whole night."

- "I get anxious at the prospect of having nothing to do."

- "I get rigid when making plans; it's difficult for me to 'go with the flow.'"

- "My life is out of balance; it's all work."

- "This belief keeps me from spending more time with my children."

Claire then examined the advantages and disadvantages to see how realistic they were. She realized that her productivity probably wouldn't be curtailed if she took more time out for herself along the way. She even conceded that building more pleasure into her day might recharge her for her work, which often became tedious and burdensome. The advantage of "finding meaning" in her work was the most difficult for her to see in another way. But she also realized that this advantage fed into a parallel and more harmful belief, that she was worthless if she didn't justify her existence by keeping busy all the time.

Rate your mood. Before starting the next exercise, rate your mood on a scale from 1 to 10, in which 1 means "miserable" and 10 means "good": _____ .

EXERCISE: Explore the Pros and Cons of Your Belief

1. Take the thought that you examined in the previous exercise that represents a barrier for you. Then list all the advantages and disadvantages of believing this thought.

    a. Advantages:

    _____

    _____

    _____

    b. Disadvantages:

    _____

    _____

    _____

Examine the Advantages

In this part of the exercise, you'll look point by point at the advantages of believing this thought. How valid is each point? Can you introduce a new perspective so that each supposed advantage no longer serves as an advantage?

Advantage #1: _____

Validity: _____

Alternative Perspective: _____

_____

Advantage #2: _____

Validity: _____

Alternative Perspective: _____

_____

Advantage #3: _____

Validity: _____

Alternative Perspective: _____

_____

Advantage #4: _____

Validity: _____

Alternative Perspective: _____

_____

Advantage #5: _____

Validity: _____

Alternative Perspective: _____

_____

Advantage #6: _____

Validity: _____

Alternative Perspective: _____

_____

Advantage #7: _____

Validity: _____

Alternative Perspective: _____

_____

Advantage #8: _____

Validity: _____

Alternative Perspective: _____

_____

Advantage #9: _____

Validity: _____

Alternative Perspective: _____

_____

Advantage #10: _____

Validity: _____

Alternative Perspective: _____

_____

After doing this work, how many valid advantages do you have? How does this list compare in length to the disadvantages? If you're interested in changing the belief behind this thought, you can explore the process of what changing might entail in the next section.

Rerate your mood. Rate on a scale from 1 to 10 (in which 10 means "fine") how you feel now: _____ . How does this number differ from your initial rating? How do you account for any changes?

_____

_____

_____

_____

EXAMINING THE ADVANTAGES AND DISADVANTAGES OF CHANGING YOUR BELIEF

In this section, similar to when you looked at the pros and cons of changing any of your unhealthy behaviors, you can look at the advantages and disadvantages of changing your belief.

Selma examined her belief that life had no meaning.

Advantages of changing this belief:

* "I'd feel happier if I knew that life had meaning."

* "I'd feel more satisfaction with what I'm doing."

* "I'd spend more time doing worthwhile activities."

Disadvantages of changing:

* "It might feel uncomfortable to change."

* "I'm not sure how to change."

* "I won't have an excuse anymore not to do anything."

The disadvantages Selma named are nearly universal to changing all kinds of negative thoughts. The first disadvantage she named, the discomfort involved with change, is almost an inevitable part of the process. Typically, it takes about three weeks to break a habit, and an outworn belief system can be considered a habitual way of thinking. Remind yourself that it takes time and practice to change a belief system; I'll discuss strategies for doing so in the next section. The second disadvantage Selma identified, being unsure how to change, can be tackled by the skill of brainstorming, which you first practiced in chapter 3. This workbook has also pointed out various other strategies for change that you can implement, and the next section explores how you can change your beliefs.

Selma decided to brainstorm about how to make her life more meaningful:

- Change jobs.

- Find a group-oriented hobby.

- Join a hiking club.

- Pick up a volunteer job.

- Foster a child from the local child welfare department.

- Move to a foreign country and do volunteer work.

- Visit a spiritual advisor.

- Go to a new church.

- Pray every day.

- Go to graduate school.

- Go on a retreat vacation.

- Train for a walking or biking holiday.

- Train for a marathon.

Selma decided to implement several of these alternatives. She decided that she could easily visit a new church; she could also search the Internet for walking vacations in Europe. She thought it would be easier to stick to her regime of walking for exercise if there was a larger purpose than just doing it to get in shape. Taking a vacation once she'd met her walking goals seemed like a good reward.

Rate your mood. Before starting the next exercise, rate your mood on a scale from 1 to 10, in which 1 means "miserable" and 10 means "good": _____ .

EXERCISE: Explore Advantages and Disadvantages of Changing Your Belief

Recalling the process of brainstorming, without censoring yourself come up with as many different ideas as you can about how to solve a particular problem. Don't worry about selecting any of the ideas right now; just be concerned with generating as long a list as possible.

Advantages of changing this belief:

_____

_____

_____

_____

_____

Disadvantages of changing this belief:

_____

_____

_____

_____

_____

Now brainstorm about possible ways you can change your belief.

Ways to change your belief:

_____

_____

_____

_____

_____

Out of these possible ways to change your belief, circle the ones that seem to be viable alternatives for you to implement.

Rerate your mood. Rate on a scale from 1 to 10 (in which 10 means "fine") how you feel now: _____ . How does this number differ from your initial rating? How do you account for any changes?

_____

_____

_____

_____

CHANGING YOUR THOUGHTS

The final step in cognitive restructuring is to substitute your distorted beliefs with thinking that serves you better. Usually you can do this by turning the belief on its tail and changing it into its opposite. Louis turned his negative belief, "My life is hopeless," to "I'm filled with hope." A stumbling block occurs for some people in that the opposite thought may sound exorbitant and unrealistic. For instance, Matthew berated himself for making mistakes in his new job by saying, "I'm such a loser." The opposite thought, "I'm a winner," sounded artificial to him. In such instances, you may want to scale back the thought to a statement that's more moderate in nature, such as, "It takes everyone a while to get used to a new job."

Sometimes it's hard working with thoughts, because they're abstract notions; we can't actually see or feel them. The following exercise, a variation of the scaling questions explored in chapter 3, is designed to work with thoughts at a more concrete level. The steps for using the scale in this way are as follows:

1. Rephrase your negative belief as a positive statement. To counter his negative belief that his life had no hope, Louis chose as his new belief, "My life has meaning."

2. To determine how much you believe in this new statement, create a scale in which 10 means that you believe it wholeheartedly, and 1 means that you don't believe it at all.

3. Rate where you currently stand: _____ . What three actions are you taking, and what are you saying to yourself to get to this place?

Action #1:

_____

_____

_____

_____

Action #2:

_____

_____

_____

_____

Action #3:

_____

_____

_____

_____

Louis rated his belief in the positive statement at 1 on the scale from 1 to 10. In the event that you're at 1, list three actions you're taking to prevent things from getting even worse.

Sample Action #1: Louis said he keeps going to work every day and working as late as necessary to get everything done.

Sample Action #2: Louis talks to his girlfriend about what's going on with him, and she's good at listening.

Sample Action #3: Louis has attended a couple of AA meetings in the past and is considering going again.

In the event you rated your belief at 1 on the scale, what will you do to make sure that things don't get worse?

Action #1:

_____

_____

_____

_____

Action #2:

_____

_____

_____

_____

Action #3:

_____

_____

_____

_____

Louis realized that he was doing quite a bit and perhaps wasn't completely at 1. He had emotional support, and still valued his work commitments. He also had drawn on AA as a support resource in the past, and would consider it again.

4. Ask yourself how an important person in your life would rate your belief in your positive statement on the scale. You can either ask that person or guess how he or she might rate your belief.

    Louis speculated that his girlfriend might put him at 4 on the scale. He said that sometimes she'd felt like giving up on him too, but most of the time, she'd tried to help him.

5. Ask yourself what you can do to move your level of belief up the scale toward 10. Louis decided that he'd look into getting a transfer at work, so he could live in a different city, far from his social network with whom he did drugs. He thought that in a new place, he might feel more hopeful about his potential to change his behavior.

By working through these steps, people often find that they move past the dichotomous thinking that underlies cognitive distortions and leads to problem behaviors. Rather than seeing that there was no hope, Louis saw that he was taking several actions, now or in the past, that seemed to indicate that his life did have hope. He also realized that there might be more options for change.

Rate your mood: Rate your mood on a scale from 1 to 10 here: _____ .

EXERCISE: Use Scaling Intervention to Change Beliefs

1. Construct a 1-to-10 scale of your new belief phrased as a positive statement. What's the new belief? *Example:* Janelle, a single parent, said she wanted to believe, "I'm as worthwhile as anyone else."

_____

_____

_____

_____

2. List three actions you'd be doing if you could rate your new belief at 10 on the scale. For example, if a camera were to record your every daily action, how much would this belief be apparent in your actions? *Example:* Janelle came up with these indicators: (1) "I'd stand up for myself." (2) "I'd set limits with my child." (3) "I'd do things for myself."

Action #1:

_____

_____

_____

Action #2:

_____

_____

_____

_____

Action #3:

_____

_____

_____

_____

3. Rank your progress using the scale you've created. How have you been able to get to this point? (If you rank your progress at 1, what can you do to make sure that things don't get even worse?) *Example:* Janelle said she was at 2 on the scale, because she does try to discipline her child.

_____

_____

_____

_____

4. Where would somebody who knows you well rate your belief on this scale? *Example:* Janelle said, "My best friend would say that I was at 1, that I need to stand up for myself, although she's one of the people I should stand up to."

_____

_____

_____

_____

5. What three actions can you take to move your level of belief up the scale toward 10? *Example:* (1) Janelle could go out with a friend once a week while her son stays with a babysitter. (2) Janelle said, "I could have my son go to bed at eight o'clock so I can have time for myself in the evenings." (3) She determined, "I can ask my supervisor to avoid giving me work at the last minute so that I can be on time for my child's after-school care."

Action #1:

_____

_____

_____

_____

Action #2:

_____

_____

_____

_____

Action #3:

_____

_____

_____

_____

Rerate your mood. On a scale from 1 to 10 (in which 10 means "fine"), rate your overall mood now: _____ . How does this number differ from the rating you gave yourself just before starting this exercise? How do you account for any changes?

_____

_____

_____

_____

HELPFUL SELF-TALK

Up until now in this chapter, I've focused on how to identify and change unhelpful thinking. While reducing unhelpful thinking is important, happiness researcher Martin Seligman claims that having positive thoughts is more important than decreasing negative thoughts. In fact, he suggests that people should have twice the number of positive thoughts as negative ones (Seligman 2004). You may be turned off by the term "positive," because it may have Pollyanna connotations for you. I'll stick with the term "helpful" here, meaning thoughts that serve you in feeling better.

Rate your mood. Before you explore how to increase your helpful thinking, please rate your mood here on a scale from 1 to 10: _____ .

EXERCISE: List Your Helpful Thoughts

Throughout this book, the various exercises have asked you to record the statements you make to motivate yourself, help yourself feel better, or make situations more manageable for you. Go through the chapters and compile here all your helpful, optimistic, or hopeful thoughts or beliefs into a single list.

_____

_____

_____

_____

_____

_____

_____

_____

_____

Rerate your mood. Rate on a scale from 1 to 10 (in which 10 means "fine") how you feel now: _____ . How does this number differ from your initial rating? How do you account for any changes?

_____

_____

_____

_____

EXERCISE: "Catch" Yourself Having Helpful Thoughts

Another way of tracking your helpful thoughts involves a variation of an earlier exercise in which you listed your unhelpful thinking. Over the next day, "catch" yourself having helpful thoughts. They can range from fleeting thoughts ("The weather's nice") to more broad-ranging concerns: "This is a difficult period right now, because I've had a lot of stress all at once, but this will pass pretty soon, and the situation will resolve itself." Or they might be as follows: "I've done what I can in this situation, and now I'll just have to trust that things will work out. They usually do." These thoughts don't have to be about you; they can also be about other people or your surroundings.

Thought #1:

_____

_____

_____

_____

Thought #2:

_____

_____

_____

_____

Thought #3:

_____

_____

_____

_____

Thought #4:

_____

_____

_____

_____

Thought #5:

_____

_____

_____

_____

Rerate your mood. Rate on a scale from 1 to 10 (in which 10 means "fine") how you feel now: _____ . How does this number differ from your initial rating? How do you account for any changes?

_____

_____

_____

_____

EXERCISE: Create Two Helpful Thoughts for Each Unhelpful One

In line with Seligman's guidelines for the proportion of positive to negative thoughts, "catch" yourself when you have unhelpful thoughts over the next day, then replace them with two helpful statements each. For example, Samantha mentioned that a coworker had said she looked tired. Her unhelpful thought was: "I must look really ugly."

Her two helpful thoughts were:

- "I enjoyed staying up last night to watch that movie, even though I'm a bit tired today."

- "My coworker sounded concerned about me."

Unhelpful thought:

_____

_____

_____

Helpful thought #1:

_____

_____

_____

Helpful thought #2:

_____

_____

_____

Unhelpful thought:

_____

_____

_____

Helpful thought #1:

_____

_____

_____

Helpful thought #2:

_____

_____

_____

Unhelpful thought:

_____

_____

_____

Helpful thought #1:

_____

_____

_____

Helpful thought #2:

_____

_____

_____

Unhelpful thought:

_____

_____

_____

Helpful thought #1:

_____

_____

_____

Helpful thought #2:

_____

_____

_____

Unhelpful thought:

_____

_____

_____

Helpful thought #1:

_____

_____

_____

Helpful thought #2:

_____

_____

_____

Unhelpful thought:

_____

_____

_____

Helpful thought #1:

_____

_____

_____

Helpful thought #2:

_____

_____

_____

Unhelpful thought:

_____

_____

_____

Helpful thought #1:

_____

_____

_____

Helpful thought #2:

_____

_____

_____

Unhelpful thought:

_____

_____

_____

Helpful thought #1:

_____

_____

_____

Helpful thought #2:

_____

_____

_____

Unhelpful thought:

_____

_____

_____

Helpful thought #1:

_____

_____

_____

Helpful thought #2:

_____

_____

_____

Unhelpful thought:

_____

_____

_____

Helpful thought #1:

_____

_____

_____

Helpful thought #2:

_____

_____

_____

Rerate your mood. Rate on a scale from 1 to 10 (in which 10 means "fine") how you feel now: _____ . How does this number differ from your initial rating? How do you account for any changes?

_____

_____

_____

_____

CONCLUSION

This chapter has focused on how to both decrease unhelpful thinking and increase helpful thinking. If you've worked through the different exercises, you've probably become more flexible in your thinking and realized that your thoughts aren't "cast in stone," nor do they define you. You can work with them to harness them as a powerful resource that works better for you. Hopefully, by doing the exercises, you've also become more aware of any unhelpful thoughts you have that foster your depression. Most important, through your work, hopefully you've identified methods that succeed for you in changing your thoughts so that your mood improves.

CHAPTER 9

Building Relationships

This chapter focuses on building your interpersonal skills. One theme of this workbook has been the importance of social support for bolstering mood and preventing depression. If you improve how you relate to other people, you can increase the number of people available to you, and the quality of the support. Being able to talk to others about problems sometimes generates new perspectives. Additionally, sharing your painful feelings with others can help you cope with them. Socializing can also be a way to have more enjoyment in your life. Having relationships with others also helps protect you against the negative effects of stressful life events. Finally, relationships with others often provide the meaning in life for which depressed people yearn.

Since interpersonal stress can trigger depression, learning how to deal with these situations is important, not only to increase the strengths and protections you have available but also to reduce your risk of becoming depressed. Knowing what to say and how to say it when encountering troubling periods in relationships will help you feel more confident, rather than hopeless, about handling conflict when it inevitably arises. This chapter delves into some of the strategies for enhancing relationships, which include building social and communication skills.

SOCIAL SKILLS

This section applies to those who feel awkward around other people: "I don't know what to say. Other people seem as if they can talk to others, but I can't." But being able to talk to other people is a skill that can be learned. Most people aren't born with it and have to be taught how to do it. This chapter offers these essential skills broken down into their basic parts: greeting someone, starting a conversation, listening, and asking questions. The exercises invite you to practice these new skills in real-life situations.

Greeting Someone

The first skill is to greet people in a way that conveys that you're glad to see them. Specifically, saying "hello" and smiling are essential behaviors here. You might not feel like smiling because you feel depressed, but it tells other people that you're friendly and interested in getting to know them.

Rate your mood. Rate your mood now on a scale from 1 to 10: _____ .

EXERCISE: Practice Greeting People

Greet three people today by smiling and saying "hi." Briefly describe the reaction you got each time.

Person #1:

_____

_____

Person #2:

_____

_____

Person #3:

_____

_____

Rerate your mood. Rate on a scale from 1 to 10 (in which 10 means "fine") how you feel now: _____. How does this number differ from your initial rating? How do you account for any changes?

_____

_____

_____

_____

Starting a Conversation

The only thing you have to remember about starting a conversation is to look around you. Whatever's going on right then is the best topic for conversation, because that's a situation that you share in the moment with the other person. Here are some common examples that cover many potential situations:

- The weather's a perennial favorite, because it's a circumstance people share.

- If you're waiting in a line, you can talk about the wait time.

- If you're a parent with your children, and are around other parents and their children, you can talk about the children.

- If you're attending an event, you can discuss the event.

- If you're at work, you can talk about office politics, requirements, or tasks.

- If you're at a gym, you can talk about workouts, exercise gear, or the gym.

- If you're in school, you can talk about assignments, due dates, or the instructor.

Rate your mood. Rate your mood now on a scale from 1 to 10: _____.

EXERCISE: Start a Conversation

Write down three people you know from work, social activities, or other aspects of your daily life whom you could possibly start a conversation with:

Person #1:

_____

_____

Person #2:

_____

_____

Person #3:

_____

_____

Consider what you could talk about with each of these people.

Person #1:

_____

_____

Person #2:

_____

_____

Person #3:

_____

_____

Rerate your mood. Rate on a scale from 1 to 10 (in which 10 means "fine") how you feel now: _____ . How does this number differ from your initial rating? How do you account for any changes?

_____

_____

_____

_____

Listening

How do you know if someone's really listening to you? The person maintains eye contact, rather than looking around, and nods or affirms that he or she understands what you're saying. Rather than give advice when someone talks about a difficult subject, a good listener indicates that he or she empathizes with your perspective. For example, you'd say to a person who's torn about resuming her job after a period of time off, "It's a hard decision to decide to go back to work when your children are small," rather than, "I think everyone should stay home with the children." The former statement is an example of _reflective listening_, in which you paraphrase the other's position. The latter is an example of advice giving or telling someone what to do.

There are two ways to paraphrase a person's conversation. One is to reflect back the content of what he or she says: "It's really difficult in this area to find a good day care that doesn't already have a waiting list." The other is to reflect back the feeling underlying the message: "It sounds as if you're worried that your child will be in a school that has a high teacher turn-around." Paraphrasing or reflecting back someone's message is a surprisingly powerful tool to use in conversations. People feel heard and understood when you're able to convey that you understand their experience.

Rate your mood. Rate your mood now on a scale from 1 to 10: _____ .

EXERCISE: Develop Your Listening Skills

1. Recall three recent times when someone was talking to you and you could've paraphrased what he or she said, rather than saying nothing at all or giving advice (two common responses).

    Your response reflecting other's content #1:

    _____

    _____

    Your response reflecting other's content #2:

    _____

    _____

    Your response reflecting other's content #3:

    _____

    _____

2. For the sake of practice, for these three incidents think of ways you could've reflected back the other person's feelings.

    Your response reflecting other's feeling #1:

    _____

    _____

    Your response reflecting other's feeling #2:

    _____

    _____

    Your response reflecting other's feeling #3:

    _____

    _____

3. Try making a reflecting comment the next time you're in a conversation. If you've done this, what did you say?

_____

_____

_____

_____

4. What was the response?

_____

_____

_____

_____

Rerate your mood. Rate on a scale from 1 to 10 (in which 10 means "fine") how you feel now: _____ . How does this number differ from your initial rating? How do you account for any changes?

_____

_____

_____

_____

Asking Questions

Another way to let people know that you're interested in them is to ask them questions. In conversation, the best kind of question is open ended rather than closed ended. Open-ended questions are those that invite people to come up with their own responses, while closed-ended questions are those that can be answered as a one-word response (for example, "Where do you live?" "How many brothers and sisters do you have?"). Closed-ended questions, particularly when asked in a series, can start to sound like an interrogation rather than a conversation, whereas open-ended questions encourage people to more freely express their thoughts and feelings about a topic, without being constrained in a certain way.

Rate your mood. Rate your mood now on a scale from 1 to 10: _____ .

EXERCISE: Develop Your Questioning Skills

In the conversations you just recalled, what open-ended questions could you have asked (or did you ask)?

Open-ended question #1:

_____

_____

_____

Open-ended question #2:

_____

_____

_____

Open-ended question #3:

_____

_____

_____

Rerate your mood. Rate on a scale from 1 to 10 (in which 10 means "fine") how you feel now: _____. How does this number differ from your initial rating? How do you account for any changes?

_____

_____

_____

_____

DEALING WITH INTERPERSONAL STRESS

When people become closer, conflict and misunderstanding are an almost inevitable part of the process. Rather than seeing your relationship troubles as a sign that relationships "never work," "people can't be trusted," or "people are no good," you can instead see relationship difficulties as an opportunity for the relationship to go deeper, to a more authentic level. Learning some basic communication skills can give you the tools to navigate conflict more effectively. In this section, I discuss two deceptively simple techniques: using *I-messages* and asking others to change their behavior.

I-Messages

If people have hurt or mistreated you, then you can tell them how you feel through I-messages. When you use I-messages, you convey how you feel or your reaction in a certain situation, rather than blame the other person for what has happened. When people feel blamed, they're defensive and less likely to see your position or to change the way they act toward you.

The basic format for giving I-messages is this: "I feel _____ [the reaction] in response to what happened [the specific action]." Here's an example: "I feel disappointed that you didn't call," rather than, "Why didn't you call me?" If you have trouble identifying your feeling, remember that the four main feelings are angry, sad, happy, and scared.

Rate your mood. Rate on a scale from 1 to 10 (in which 10 means "fine") how you feel now: _____ .

EXERCISE: Practice Giving I-Messages

Consider three recent situations in which you could've told other people how you felt. Construct an I message for each of these situations.

I-Message #1: I feel _____ [mad, sad, scared, glad] when you _____ [other person's specific behavior].

_____

_____

I-Message #2: I feel _____ [mad, sad, scared, glad] when you _____ [other person's specific behavior].

_____

_____

I-Message #3: I feel _____ [mad, sad, scared, glad] when you _____ [other person's specific behavior].

_____

_____

Rerate your mood. Rate on a scale from 1 to 10 (in which 10 means "fine") how you feel now: _____ . How does this number differ from your initial rating? How do you account for any changes?

_____

_____

_____

_____

Asking People to Change Their Behavior

Another piece of effective communication involves learning to make clear behavior requests of others. Although the others may or may not change their behavior because you've asked them to do so, a person is most likely to change if you've made the request. Additionally, you've let the person know how you feel and how you expect to be treated. When you do this, you feel better about yourself. Your sense of self-worth is a key component feeding into your depression. Increasing your self-esteem helps improve your mood.

Here are some guidelines for making requests:

- Be specific: "Please call me if you're going to be a half-hour late," rather than global—"Can't you be considerate?"

- Make your request measurable, if possible: "I'd like for you to call me once a day."

- State your request in the form of initiating a positive behavior rather than getting rid of a negative behavior: "Give me a chance to change clothes and look over the mail when I come home," rather than, "Stop bothering me with your problems."

Rate your mood. Rate on a scale from 1 to 10 (in which 10 means "fine") how you feel now: _____ .

EXERCISE: Practice Asking for a Behavioral Change

Using the situations you used for the "Practice Giving I-Messages" exercise, construct a behavioral request for each of the three scenarios.

Behavioral change request #1:

_____

_____

Behavioral change request #2:

_____

_____

Behavioral change request #3:

_____

_____

Rerate your mood. Rate on a scale from 1 to 10 (in which 10 means "fine") how you feel now: _____ . How does this number differ from your initial rating? How do you account for any changes?

_____

_____

_____

_____

CONCLUSION

Listening effectively, speaking up for your needs by using I-messages, and clearly conveying how you want other people to behave toward you are key communication tools for navigating relationships more skillfully. Having better social skills will help you attract more people to you, and you'll likely feel better as a result of increased socializing and support. This chapter has covered some of the ways to build these important tools for relationships.

Conclusion

I hope this workbook has helped you find and enhance the supports, resources, and strengths that are available to you. I've emphasized doing what works for you when managing your depression, recognizing that you're the expert on what's most helpful for you. In keeping with this theme, you'll now be asked to reflect on what has been most helpful for you in this workbook before you build on the changes you've made.

HELPFUL EXERCISES

What three exercises in this workbook did you find most useful? What did you learn from them? Kelly found the "Focus on a Feeling" exercise in chapter 7 valuable, because she hadn't realized that her feelings played such a powerful role in her depression. Barbara understood, from examining the advantages and disadvantages of her depression (chapter 5), that she received many secondary gains from having depression. Rob identified that most of the time (while he was at work), he felt okay, and that it was only at night and on weekends that he struggled with loneliness and depression. Seeing that at least half the time he wasn't depressed, he no longer defined himself as "depressed." Instead, he saw himself as an active person who needed more things to do to fill in his time.

Helpful exercise #1:

_____

_____

_____

What you learned:

_____

_____

_____

Helpful exercise #2:

_____

_____

_____

What you learned:

_____

_____

_____

Helpful exercise #3:

_____

_____

_____

What you learned:

_____

_____

_____

What exercise did you find least helpful? How would you change the exercise so that it could be more helpful for you? What would you uncover if you'd done the exercise this way?

Least helpful exercise:

_____

_____

_____

How you would change the exercise:

_____

_____

_____

What you learned:

_____

_____

_____

STRATEGIES

What strategies in this book have you continued to use or do you plan to use? These may or may not overlap with the exercises you identified that were most helpful for you. When Kelly found herself getting too rigid in her thinking, and saw no way out, she liked to list the advantages and the disadvantages of a particular belief that fed into her depression, such as "I have to get all A's in graduate school to feel okay about myself." This freed up her thinking and helped her realize that she had options, so she didn't have to feel trapped in hopelessness. She also liked the strategy of listing at least five "I feel _____ [mad, sad, scared, or glad], because _____ [specific event]" statements when she experienced depression, to help her understand what had triggered her mood. This strategy also got her to view her depression in a different light. Rather than see it as an overwhelming, amorphous fog, she viewed her depression as triggered by a manageable incident that she could figure out how to handle. Even if she couldn't change her circumstances, it was better to know that her depression related to something tangible rather than just experience intensely negative feelings that seemed out of her control.

What strategies do you think will work well (or have already worked well) for you in managing your depression?

Strategy #1:

_____

_____

_____

Strategy #2:

_____

_____

_____

Strategy #3:

_____

_____

_____

Strategy #4:

_____

_____

_____

Strategy #5:

_____

_____

_____

PREVENTING DEPRESSIVE EPISODES

Because you have more knowledge of your triggers now from your work in chapter 7, you may be aware of what sets off a depressive episode so that you can forestall its happening or decrease its intensity. The following questions ask you to think about cues for your depression and how you could prevent them from taking hold. These techniques are drawn from solution-focused therapy (O'Hanlon and Weiner-Davis 1989). In keeping with the solution-focused view that language influences how you think about things, note that the questions suggest that further depression is not inevitable. The answers you provide are to give you some tools in place so that you can handle the depression only if it rears up again.

1. What *would* be the first thing you'd notice *if* you started to find yourself slipping back into depression?

_____

_____

_____

_____

2. What *could* you do to prevent depression from setting in any further?

_____

_____

_____

_____

Through the exercises in this workbook, you've searched and enhanced your own assets and your motivation to work on your depression. You've likely emerged from this process with an improved sense of your own capacities and taken some actions consistent with a positive shift in your perspective. After tapping into your available resources, you learned specific tools that can help you manage your depression. Through the process of building both your strengths and your skills, you've taken steps to overcome your depression and prevent it from happening in the future.

References

American Psychiatric Association. 2000. *Desk Reference to the Diagnostic Criteria from DSM-IV-TR. 4th ed., text revision.* Washington, DC: American Psychiatric Association.

Arnett, P., and J. Randolph. 2006. Longitudinal course of depression symptoms in multiple sclerosis. *Journal of Neurology, Neurosurgery, and Psychiatry* 77:606–10.

Arkowitz, H., H. Westra, W. Miller, and S. Rollnick. (Eds.) 2008. *Motivational Interviewing in the Treatment of Psychological Problems.* NY: Guilford Publications.

Beardslee, W. R., E. M. Versage, and T. R. Gladstone. 1998. Children of affectively ill parents: A review of the past 10 years. *Journal of the American Academy of Child and Adolescent Psychiatry* 37 (11):1134–41.

Berg, I. K. 1994. *Family Based Services: A Solution-Focused Approach.* 1st ed. New York: W. W. Norton & Company.

Bertolino, B., and B. O'Hanlon. 2002. *Collaborative, Competency-Based Counseling and Therapy.* Boston: Allyn & Bacon.

Bockting, C. L., P. Spinhoven, M. W. Koeter, L. F. Wouters, and A. H. Schene—Depression Evaluation Longitudinal Therapy Assessment Study Group. 2006. Prediction of recurrence in recurrent depression and the influence of consecutive episodes on vulnerability for depression: A 2-year prospective study. *Journal of Clinical Psychiatry* 67 (5):747–55.

Bonomi, A. E., E. A. Cannon, M. L. Anderson, F. P. Rivara, and R. S. Thompson. 2008. Association between self-reported health and physical and/or sexual abuse experienced before age 18. *Child Abuse and Neglect* 32 (7):693–701.

Cade, B., and W. H. O'Hanlon. 1993. *A brief guide to brief therapy.* New York: W. W. Norton & Company, Inc.

Christensen, D. N., J. Todahl, and W. C. Barrett. 1999. *Solution-Based Casework: An Introduction to Clinical and Case Management Skills in Casework Practice.* New York: Aldine de Gruyter.

Clarke, G., and P. M. Lewinsohn. 1995. *The adolescent coping with stress class: Leader manual.* Retrieved on August 4, 2008, from www.kpchr.org/public/acwd/CWS_MANUAL.pdf.

Cuijpers, P., A. van Straten, and L. Warmerdam. 2007. Behavioral activation treatments of depression: A meta-analysis. *Clinical Psychology Review* 27 (3):318–26.

de Jong, P., and I. K. Berg. 2008. *Interviewing for Solutions.* 3rd. ed. Pacific Grove, CA: Brooks/Cole.

de Shazer, S. 1988. *Clues: Investigating solutions in brief therapy.* New York: Norton.

de Shazer, S. 1994. *Words Were Originally Magic.* New York: W. W. Norton & Company.

de Shazer, S., I. K. Berg, E. Lipchick, E. Nunnally, A. Molnar, W. Gingerich, and M. Weiner-Davis. 1986. Brief therapy: Focused solution development. *Family Process* 25(2): 207–21.

D'Zurilla, T. J., and A. M. Nezu. 2001. Problem-solving therapies. In *Handbook of Cognitive-Behavioral Therapies,* 2nd ed., edited by K. S. Dobson. New York: The Guilford Press.

Golding, J. M. 1999. Intimate partner violence as a risk factor for mental disorders: A meta-analysis. *Journal of Family Violence* 14 (2):99–132.

Goodman, S. H., and I. H. Gotlib. 1999. Risk for psychopathology in the children of depressed mothers: A developmental model for understanding mechanisms of transmission. *Psychological Review* 106 (3):458–61.

Helgeson, V. S., K. A. Reynolds, and P. L. Tomich. 2006. A meta-analytic review of benefit finding and growth. *Journal of Consulting and Clinical Psychology* 74 (5):797–816.

Holahan, C. J., R. H. Moos, C. K. Holahan, P. L. Brennan, and K. K. Schutte. 2005. Stress generation, avoidance coping, and depressive symptoms: A 10-year model. *Journal of Consulting and Clinical Psychology* 73 (4):658–66.

Kessler, R. C., P. Berglund, O. Demler, R. Jin, D. Koretz, K. R. Merikangas, A. J. Rush, E. E. Walters, and P. S. Wang. 2003. The epidemiology of major depressive disorder: Results from the National Comorbidity Survey Replication (NCS-R). *Journal of the American Medical Association* 289 (23):3095–3105.

Kraaij, V., E. Arensman, and P. Spinhoven. 2002. Negative life events and depression in elderly persons: A meta-analysis. *Journals of Gerontology: Series B—Psychological Sciences and Social Sciences* 57 (1):87–94.

McKay, M., M. Davis, and P. Fanning. 1997. *Thoughts and Feelings: Taking Control of Your Moods and Your Life*. Oakland, CA: New Harbinger Publications, Inc.

Meyers, B. S., J. A. Sirey, M. Bruce, M. Hamilton, P. Raue, S. J. Friedman, C. Rickey, T. Kakuma, M. K. Carroll, D. Kiosses, and G. Alexopoulos. 2002. Predictors of early recovery from major depression among persons admitted to community-based clinics: An observational study. *Archives of General Psychiatry* 59 (8):729–35.

Miller, W. R., and S. Rollnick. 2002. *Motivational Interviewing: Preparing People for Change.* 2nd ed. New York: The Guilford Press.

Morris, S., J. Alexander, and H. Waldron. 1988. Functional family therapy. In *Handbook of Behavioral Family Therapy*, edited by I. R. H. Falloon. New York: The Guilford Press.

Mueller, T. I., A. C. Leon, M. B. Keller, D. A. Solomon, J. Endicott, W. Coryell, M. Warshaw, and J. D. Maser. 1999. Recurrence after recovery from major depressive disorder during 15 years of observational follow-up. *American Journal of Psychiatry* 156 (7):1000–06.

Murphy, R. T. 2008. Enhancing combat veterans' motivation to change posttraumatic stress disorder symptoms and other problem behaviors. In *Motivational Interviewing in the Treatment of Psychological Problems*, edited by H. Arkowitz, H. A. Westra, W. R. Miller, and S. Rollnick. New York: The Guilford Press.

Nolen-Hoeksema, S. 2002. Gender differences in depression. In *Handbook of Depression*, 1st ed., edited by I. H. Gotlib and C. L. Hammen. New York: The Guilford Press.

Penza, K. M., C. Heim, and C. B. Nemeroff. 2006. Trauma and depression. In *Women and Depression: A Handbook for the Social, Behavioral, and Biomedical Sciences*, edited by C. L. M. Keyes and S. H. Goodman. New York: Cambridge University Press.

Pilowsky, D. J., P. J. Wickramaratne, A. J. Rush, C. W. Hughes, J. Garber, E. Malloy, C. A. King, G. Cerda, A. B. Sood, J. E. Alpert, S. R. Wisniewski, M. H. Trivedi, A. Talati, M. M. Carlson, H. H. Liu, M. Fava, and M. M. Weissman. 2006. Children of currently depressed mothers: A STAR*D ancillary study. *Journal of Clinical Psychiatry* 67 (1):126–36.

Prochaska, J. O., J. C. Norcross, and C. C. DiClemente. 1994. *Changing for Good: A Revolutionary Six-Stage Program for Overcoming Bad Habits and Moving Your Life Positively Forward.* New York: Avon Books.

Rugulies, R. 2002. Depression as a predictor for coronary heart disease: A review and meta-analysis. *American Journal of Preventive Medicine* 23 (1):51–61.

Rush, A., M. Trivedi, S. Wisniewski, et al. 2006. Bupropion-SR, sertraline, or venlafaxine-XR after failure of SSRI's for depression. *New England Journal of Medicine* 354:1231-42.

Seligman, M. E. P. 2004. *Authentic Happiness: Using the New Positive Psychology to Realize Your Potential for Lasting Fulfillment.* Paperback ed. New York: The Free Press.

Sullivan, P. F., M. C. Neale, and K. S. Kendler. 2000. Genetic epidemiology of major depression: Review and meta-analysis. *American Journal of Psychiatry* 157:1552–62.

Treasure, J., and U. Schmidt. 2008. Motivational Interviewing in the Management of Eating Disorders. In *Motivational Interviewing in the Treatment of Psychological Problems*, edited by H. Arkowitz, H. A. Westra, W. R. Miller, and S. Rollnick. New York: The Guilford Press.

Trivedi, M. H., A. J. Rush, S. R. Wisniewski, A. A. Nierenberg, D. Warden, L. Ritz, G. Norquist, R. H. Howland, B. Lebowitz, P. J. McGrath, K. Shores-Wilson, M. M. Biggs, G. K. Balasubramani, and M. Fava—STAR*D Study Team. 2006. Evaluation of outcomes with citalopram for depression using measurement-based care in STAR*D: Implications for clinical practice. *American Journal of Psychiatry* 163 (1):28–40.

Westra, H. A., and D. J. A. Dozois. 2008. Integrating motivational interviewing into the treatment of anxiety. In *Motivational Interviewing in the Treatment of Psychological Problems*, edited by H. Arkowitz, H. A. Westra, W. R. Miller, and S. Rollnick. New York: The Guilford Press.

Yalom, I. D., and M. Leszcz. 2005. *The Theory and Practice of Group Psychotherapy.* 5th ed. New York: Basic Books.

Young, J. E. 1999. *Cognitive Therapy for Personality Disorders: A Schema-Focused Approach.* 3rd ed. Sarasota, FL: Professional Resource Press.

Young, J. E., J. L. Rygh, A. D. Weinberger, and A. T. Beck. 2007. Cognitive therapy for depression. In *Clinical Handbook of Psychological Disorders: A Step-by-Step Treatment Manual*, 4th ed., edited by D. H. Barlow. New York: The Guilford Press.

Jacqueline Corcoran, Ph.D., is a professor at the Virginia Commonwealth University School of Social Work in Alexandria, VA. She has authored and coauthored many books on evidence and strengths-based models, including *Clinical Applications of Evidence-Based Family Interventions, Clinical Assessment and Diagnosis in Social Work Practice,* and *Building Strengths and Skills.*

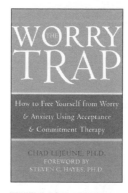
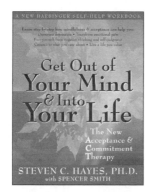
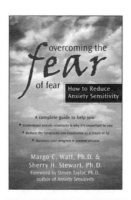